Developing Talents

Careers for Individuals with Asperger Syndrome and High-Functioning Autism

Developing Talents

Careers for Individuals with Asperger Syndrome and High-Functioning Autism

Temple Grandin and Kate Duffy

Foreword by Tony Attwood

APC

Autism Asperger Publishing Co.
P.O. Box 23173
Shawnee Mission, KS 66283-0173

©2004 Autism Asperger Publishing Co.
P.O. Box 23173
Shawnee Mission, KS 66283-0173
www.asperger.net

Publisher's Cataloging-in-Publication
(Provided by Quality Books, Inc.)

Grandin, Temple.
    Developing talents : careers for individuals with
Asperger syndrome and high-functioning autism/Temple
Grandin and Kate Duffy.
    p. cm.
    Includes bibliographical references.
    Library of Congress Control Number: 2004102676
    ISBN: 1-93-1282-56-0

    1. People with mental disabilities—Vocational
guidance. 2. Asperger's syndrome—Patients—Vocational
guidance. 3. Austism—Patients—Vocational guidance.
I. Duffy, Kate, 1953- II. Title.

HV3005.G73 2004   331.7'02'084
                                   QBI04-200107

This book is designed in Legault, Futura Condensed and Stone Sans

Managing Editor: Kirsten McBride
Cover Design: Vivian Strand

Printed in the United States of America

Foreword

A relatively small proportion of adults with Asperger Syndrome or high-functioning autism achieve long-term employment appropriate to their intellectual ability and qualifications. This is a remarkable waste of potential talent. The American workforce needs the benefit of the qualities of people with Asperger Syndrome and autism.

Temple Grandin is a pioneer in terms of her ability to achieve highly successful employment, capitalizing on the very qualities associated with autism spectrum disorders. This book is somewhat like Temple herself: practical, knowledgeable and positive. Together with Kate Duffy, a specialist in career planning, she has written a book that will be of great value to parents, teachers and employment agencies, as well as adults with high-functioning autism and Asperger Syndrome.

The book provides advice and illustrations from Temple's own experiences as well as the advice of other adults with autism or Asperger Syndrome who have also achieved lucrative and enjoyable careers. While the benefits in income and independence from successful employment are obvious, I would add that there is another important benefit. As a clinician, I have noted that adults with Asperger Syndrome tend to define themselves by their employment rather than their social network. In other words, their self-esteem is based on the quality of their work. Not surprisingly, therefore, one of the causes of depression in this population is a lack of successful and enjoyable employment. This book has the potential to significantly improve the quality of life of people with high-functioning autism and Asperger Syndrome, their families and society.

Professor Tony Attwood
March 2004

Preface

*T*his book has been a collaborative project, one that grew out of a chance meeting between Temple Grandin and Kirsten McBride, the project's editor, at a conference in 2002. The two began talking about Dr. Grandin's frustration with how few people on the autism spectrum hold down a job or are under-employed. If they only developed their talents they would have an easier time finding work, she insisted. I would like to write about it, but I don't have the time, she added.

This is where I come into the picture. I have written about careers for the past 12 years and have taught career planning and research to hundreds of college students in that time. I like helping people figure out jobs that are a good fit for them; that mean something to them. So I came into this project with a healthy respect for the step-by-step process of discovering who we are and what we do best. Yet, the real clincher for me was that maybe what Dr. Grandin and I wrote together would help my two sons, both of whom have sensory inte-gration disorder and some definite autistic traits. I was begin-ning to be up nights worrying about their futures, about what their lives would be like when they were grown.

I can say now that I don't worry as much, that working on this project has opened my eyes to a better future for my boys. I know that other parents have been in this place before, that there is strength in all of us with our deep love and concern for the welfare of our children.

And, so, that is how this book came about. Dr. Grandin and I merged our expertise and out of that collaboration a book has been birthed that, I hope, brings you and your family as much peace of mind as it has to me.

Kate Duffy
Kansas City, Missouri

Contents

Introduction

Whenever I attend autism conferences, I am struck by how many people on the high end of the autism spectrum are either unemployed or underemployed. This really bothers me because working is such an important part of my life. Without work, no matter how big or small the job, life would become small and unsatisfying for me. With work, we discover we can give back to our family and community that have given so much to us.

Yet, I realize that the idea that people with autism spectrum disorders can work in a meaningful job sounds unrealistic to many. But as someone with autism who has run a freelance livestock equipment design business and held down a part-time college professor job for over a decade, I know it can be done, and, I believe, should be done. For one, we do not want our autism to be the whole of our lives. That is neither healthy nor wise. I think that people who are able should get out in the community and get jobs.

Just as important, society loses out if individuals with autism spectrum disorders are not involved in the world of work or make other kinds of contributions to society. Some of our world's finest minds, inventions, art, and ideas belong to people with autistic traits. Albert Einstein and Vincent Van Gogh, for example, both had developmental abnormalities during early childhood, as explored in my earlier book *Thinking in Pictures* (1995). Autism is an early-onset disorder, and such characteristics as delayed speech and odd behaviors must show up before age three for a person to receive a diagnosis of autism. To be classified as having Asperger Syndrome, which is at the milder end of the autism spectrum, the child demonstrates no obvious speech delay but pronounced social skills deficits, including being a loner who is usually teased for being odd. These kids are often the really bright science "nerds." Einstein, for one, did not associate with his peers at

> Society loses out if individuals with autism spectrum disorders are not involved in the world of work or make other kinds of contributions to society.

Often, individuals on the autism spectrum do not do well in school.

school. He had tremendous single-mindedness in solving problems – but only those that interested him!

Oddly enough, it may have been that very social backwardness that led Einstein to develop his theory of relativity. After all, how many "normal" adults spend a lot of time thinking about the problems of space and time? As an adult, Einstein continued to demonstrate the traits of someone with mild autism, or Asperger Syndrome. He cared little for social niceties, wore disheveled clothes and kept his hair long and unruly. His students and colleagues reported that his lectures were scattered and sometimes incomprehensible. Often he would stop in the middle of writing a theorem on the board, seem to go into a trance, and then emerge from it a few minutes later only to write a new hypothesis (Clark, 1971).

Similarly, biographers describe artist Vincent Van Gogh as an odd, aloof child who threw many tantrums and preferred spending time alone. He was ill groomed and blunt, and spoke with tension and a nervous rasp in his voice, quite common for adults with autistic tendencies. He was also terribly self-absorbed when he spoke with others and cared little about his listeners' interest or comfort, according to Grant (1968).

Often, individuals on the autism spectrum do not do well in school. I had a horrible time graduating from high school myself. Many renowned scientists, artists and writers also had difficulties in school. For example, Gregor Mendel, the father of modern genetics, could not pass the exam to get a high school teaching license. He conducted his experiments in the corner of a monastery garden with pea plants. When he presented the results of his experiments at his thesis defense, he failed to get his degree. Nobody paid any attention to his ideas, but thankfully 120 copies of his paper survived and were recognized as the works of genius that they are after his death. Even though sometimes subject to debate, today, Mendel's principles are taught in every high school science class (Kevin, 1967).

Philosopher Ludwig Wittgenstein probably had high-functioning autism, suggests neurologist Oliver Sacks (1995). He did not talk until he was four years old, and was considered a dullard with no talent. Other members of his family presumably suffered from depression, quite common among individuals with autism spectrum disorders. Indeed, both of his brothers committed suicide. Among his talents, Wittgenstein had strong mechanical abilities, building a sewing machine at the age of 10. He used formal language, even with his peers, who teased him about his odd speech and mannerisms. We now know that overly formal speech is common in individuals on the autism spectrum.

As these examples illustrate, if we leave out certain people from society's work, we all lose out. Other famous people who were probably on the autism spectrum include Thomas Jefferson, Carl Sagan, and Amadeus Mozart (Ledgin, 2001).

For those on the autism spectrum, finding a satisfying job also provides social opportunities through shared interests. Some of the most satisfying experiences in my life have been interacting with engineers and the people I worked with to build the facilities I had designed. It was one "techie" communicating with another "techie."

Work is more than just a livelihood or paycheck; it is the key to a satisfying and productive life. For many on the autism spectrum, it is the glue that keeps our lives together in an otherwise frustrating and sometimes confusing world. Certainly, my life would not be worth living if I did not have intellectually satisfying work.

On a related note, I remember reading a few years ago about free Linux software. People in the business world had difficulty comprehending why the programmers gave their work away. But it's not a mystery to me why they would download their programs, their "ideas," into the great and evolving computer operating system. How wonderful to know your thoughts and work live on as part of the "genetic code" of a computer program. The Linux people are putting themselves into the program, contributing their "intellectual DNA" to the forever cyberspace. As the program evolves, the code they wrote will remain buried deep within it, becoming part of the great evolution of computer science. These programmers contribute to this effort because it makes their lives more meaningful.

I realize that many people on the autism spectrum, especially those with classical autism, will not go to college, or hold down a job that requires a higher education degree. Many jobs do not require a four-year college degree, but the best-paying jobs do require some formal education or training after high school. The most important thing jobs require is for the job holder to be willing to work and have a good

> For those on the autism spectrum, finding a satisfying job also provides social opportunities through shared interests.

The most important thing jobs require is for the job holder to be willing to work and have a good attitude at work.

attitude at work. In other words, be willing to learn new skills, get along with coworkers, and do the best job you can. Many people with Asperger Syndrome do well in college, for example, but have problems keeping a job upon graduation. This book will provide information that will help you develop your talents and get and keep a good job.

Even people on the lower end of the autism spectrum can work if they are coached along the way and eased into the workplace. In a way, I am my work, which provides a much-needed framework for my life. Because of my work as a livestock facilities designer and an animal science professor, I have regular and frequent contact with other people. We discuss projects, plan programs, and brainstorm ideas. Yet, I spend most of my weekend time alone, drawing and reading. If it weren't for my job, I'm afraid I would spend even more of my time secluded, isolated from the world I now navigate with some ease. This ease was hard won, and only came because of the many interventions and support I received over the years. These form the basis for the ideas and suggestions in this book

As I look back, my mother made sure I received speech therapy, a good preschool education, and a lot of help at home with social skills and manners at an early age. I was not motivated to study in high school because the subjects seemed boring to me. Biology class and working on construction projects were my main interest. Luckily, my high school science teacher used my interests to motivate me to study. We did interesting science projects, and in the process I realized I had to study "the boring stuff" to reach my goal of becoming a scientist.

Mentors were another important influence in my life and career. My high school science teacher mentored me, even into college, and several employers mentored me at my first jobs. When my anxieties grew overwhelming, I turned to medication that helped me stay on an even keel. I realize that medication is not the answer for everyone. Yet, all of the above – and more – have allowed me to continue the work I love.

As long as the livestock industry continues to use the handling facilities and equipment I have designed for the past 30 years, my thoughts live and my life has meaning. If my efforts to improve the treatment of cattle and pigs make real improvement in the world, my life is meaningful.

This book was born out of my frustration and fear that many on the autism spectrum were missing out on the very important experience of work. I feared they would never know the satisfaction of contributing to their families and their communities, of being independent and economically self-sufficient.

To build success, parents should help their children develop their natural talents. Often, these talents are the first steps toward a paying job later on. Drawing, writing, building models, programming computers or landscaping yards – all of these can grow into paying jobs. Talent speaks for itself and can sell itself, if given a chance and a decent portfolio.

Parents must also help young people learn the skills needed to find and keep a job. These skills are first learned at home. In hindsight, I was lucky to be a child of the 1950s. The more structured life style that was prevalent then was very helpful to me. For example, meals with the entire family provided opportunities to learn social skills. Other helpful activities included playing lots of board games and card games where, among other things, I learned to take turns. I was expected to sit still through dinner, to be polite to others, to do my chores, and to get along with my siblings. As I grew older, I was expected to work. At age 13, I held down my first job, working two afternoons a week as a seamstress' assistant.

Although my parents provided plenty of assistance for me, they also had high expectations. It is those expectations that have helped me navigate the world. For youths on the autism spectrum, this is especially important because they will have to work harder to prove themselves in our fast-paced, competitive global economy. The good news is that with the tremendous labor shortage facing the United States when the baby boomers retire in the next 5-10 years, employers will look more to those of us with disabilities to fill jobs for which we once would not have been considered.

Finally, young people need a mentor to give them guidance and valuable experience. Mentors introduce their protégées to the world, helping them find ways to navigate the sometimes confusing byways that life presents. After the initial introduction, they also help their protégées stay on track and develop their talents by serving as the sounding board for ideas, plans, and dreams.

This book is designed to take readers – those on the autism spectrum and their family members, teachers, counselors, and

To build success, parents should help their children develop their natural talents.

Young
people
need a
mentor to
give them
guidance
and valuable
experience.

other adults who make a difference in young lives – through the career planning process. It includes information on discovering and growing the talents and interests that might lead to satisfying work as well as a career planning and job search process. These are ideas that have helped me succeed.

Chapter 1, *Autism Spectrum Disorders and Their Effect in the Workplace*, includes:

▶ A discussion of the characteristics of autism spectrum disorders (ASD) as they relate to the workplace.

Chapter 2, *Easing into the Workplace*, focuses on:

▶ Sensory issues, anger management, medications
▶ Advice on developing and using social skills on the job
▶ Information about organizational skills to help you thrive on the job.

Chapter 3, *Rules for Success on the Job*, describes the strategies and skills you need to acquire to help make your work life more successful and fulfilling.

Chapter 4, *Finding a Vocation You Love*, is a young people's guide to finding a vocation that will not only feed their souls but also help put food on the table.

In Chapter 5, *Searching for an Ideal Job*, you'll find information about the job search process.

Chapter 6, *Do What You Do Best*, lists jobs that are particularly appropriate for the different ways of thinking that characterize those of us on the autism spectrum:

▶ visual thinkers
▶ music/math brains
▶ nonvisual thinkers with verbal brains

Chapter 7, *Best Jobs for Individuals on the Autism Spectrum*, consists of profiles of careers and jobs suited for individuals on the autism spectrum as well as information about entrepreneurship.

Finally, the book concludes with an appendix that consists of:

▶ References and resources
▶ Information on employees' legal rights in the workplace under the Americans with Disabilities Act
▶ A brief discussion on self-disclosure in the workplace
▶ Job search tips.

I hope you will find this information useful as you begin your job search or business exploration. Good luck to you and happy job-hunting.

CHAPTER 1

Autism Spectrum Disorders and Their Effect in the Workplace

As mentioned earlier, I had my first paying job during the summer when I was 13 years old. It was my mother's idea. I was moping around the house a lot, so she sent me to work two afternoons a week for her friend, a seamstress, who needed an extra set of hands in her business.

It was a perfect fit, for I loved to sew and loved to create the designs I saw in my head. I had been sewing for several years and was put to work doing the basics, ripping out seams and hemming pants. Going to work was the best thing for me; I had less time to mope and more time to learn how to negotiate the outside world.

That early work experience was exactly what I needed, and, frankly, what all of us on the autism spectrum need in order to achieve balance and success in our lives. Work is such a big part of the human experience that it's important for all to hold a job, no matter how big or small. We learn so much from working that it would be a shame to miss out on those experiences. For example, working teaches us how to get along with other people who are not part of our family; it helps us to become independent in our adult years; and it can give great satisfaction to know we are contributing to our own, as well as our family's well-being.

My job with the seamstress helped me become more independent and learn how to relate to others outside my small world of family and school. But sending me to work at age 13 was just one of a long list of interventions my mother

We learn so much from working that it would be a shame to miss out on those experiences.

It is by developing our talents that we can step more easily into the work world and find jobs that are a good fit for us.

created for me, starting with preschool and speech therapy.

Independence did not come easy, but I learned it because my family expected me to. The first two chapters of this book take a hard look at the challenges those with autism spectrum disorders (ASD) may face in the workplace and some tried-and-true interventions and solutions. These interventions can free us up so we can develop our talents and live fuller, more gratifying lives. It is by developing our talents that we can step more easily into the work world and find jobs that are a good fit for us. Sewing, for me, was one of those talents, and I'm forever thankful to my mother's friend for taking me on as a helper. That job helped me learn work skills.

At the same time, my family also enrolled me in a boarding school that had a farm, which nurtured my love of animals. I spent much of my teen years showing horses at 4-H fairs. Sewing and animal care may sound like an odd combination of hobbies, but I loved them both, and they led me to my present occupation as an animal scientist. In high school, I used my sewing skills to make fancy decorated halters and bridles for the horses.

During my five years at boarding school, I also worked on shingling the barn roof and building a new addition on the house. I loved construction work. Both sewing and construction work require visual thinking skills and putting things together. For the first four years, I seldom studied until I was motivated by Mr. Carlock, the science teacher, who, as mentioned, became one of my most important mentors.

My interest in livestock facilities began after I spent a summer on my aunt Brecheen's ranch in Arizona. I grew fixated on the equipment used to hold the cattle while they received injections or brandings. That fixation led me to into a career that I still care very much about, some 40 years later.

I do not mean to make my entry into the work world sound easy. It has not been. What I have noticed about those on the autism spectrum who successfully hold down jobs is that we share three characteristics:

▶ Somebody helped us develop our birthright talents.

▶ We had mentors during our teen and later years who helped us develop both social and job-related professional skills.

▶ Where appropriate, we took medication or other treatments, including exercise, special diets or nutritional supplements, to help us manage our sensory problems and accompanying depression and anxiety. (I realize not everyone benefits from medication, but it is an option that should not be ruled out.)

I deeply appreciate my family's hard work in raising me with a strong work ethic, but one thing is clear: all the work ethic in the world won't help me hold down a job if I can't manage my sensory system and other challenges the autism spectrum presents.

In the following we will take a brief look at the causes and characteristics of ASD. Throughout this book, we are referring to individuals with high-functioning autism, Asperger Syndrome, and pervasive developmental disabilities not otherwise specified (PPD-NOS). This discussion of causes and characteristics is by no means exhaustive or comprehensive as many other books and scientific reports have addressed these topics in great detail. Also, for our purposes, the main focus is on those aspects of autism spectrum disorders that have the greatest bearing on entering and surviving in the workplace.

Autism: Definition and Causes

Autism is a condition that affects every family member of the person on the autism spectrum. The rigors of raising a child on the autism spectrum to a fulfilling adulthood are daunting for a very good reason: autism affects every aspect of life.

The Autism Society of America defines autism as a complex developmental disability that typically appears during the first three years of life. The autism continuum ranges from a brilliant scientist to a nonverbal individual who will always have to live under supervised conditions. Some nonverbal people will be capable of doing a job and others sim-

Autism affects every aspect of life.

Worldwide, autism appears at the same rate as in the United States, with four times as many boys suffering from it as girls.

ply are not. The result of a neurological disorder that affects the functioning of the brain, autism primarily impacts the normal development of the brain in the areas of social inter-action and communication skills. Therefore, children and adults with autism typically have difficulties in verbal and nonverbal communication, social interactions, and leisure or play activities (www.autism-society.org).

Research indicates that the brains of people with autism have abnormal underdevelopment in the limbic system that is the center of emotions (Bauman & Kemper, 1994). In the frontal cortex, there is uncontrolled overgrowth of neurons (Courchesne et al., 2001). Those brain abnormalities cause many of the autistic symptoms. The severity of the autism is related to the amount of abnormal development. The rear half of the cortex where memories are stored is relatively normal. This may explain the good memories that most peo-ple on the spectrum have.

The Centers for Disease Control and Prevention reported in 2001 that autism affected an estimated 2 to 6 per 1,000 individuals – as many as 1.5 million Americans. That figure is growing 10 to 17 percent per year, according to the U.S. Department of Education and other governmental agencies that track autism and other disabilities. With that kind of growth rate, the Autism Society of America projects that in the next decade, 4 million Americans could have some form of autism (www.autism-society.org). Worldwide, autism appears at the same rate as in the United States, with four times as many boys suffering from it as girls. And as in the United States, autism affects people of all races, incomes, ethnic groups and religions.

Because autism and Asperger Syndrome are "spectrum disorders," the symptoms appear in a wide variety of com-binations, from mild to severe. The Autism Society of America (www.autism-society.org) notes that people on the autism spectrum may act very differently from each other, even if they have the same diagnosis. For example, some are nonverbal while others are capable of communicating suc-cessfully. Some on the spectrum are sensitive to smells while others are sensitive to touch, and so on.

Researchers are still not certain what causes autism, but they do know that it is a genetic disorder involving many interacting factors. Some researchers are studying possible links between heredity, genetics, and certain medical problems such as Fragile X Syndrome. Others are investigating a possible relationship between a cluster of unstable genes that may affect brain development and cause autism. Still others are studying environmental factors such as viral infections, metabolic imbalances and exposure to certain chemicals (www.autism-society.org).

Often, family members of persons on the autism spectrum have mild autistic traits. Some of these traits include visual thinking, strong intellectual abilities, shyness, and learning disabilities. Other conditions that are often present in individuals with autism or their families are depression, anxiety, attention deficit disorder, Tourette's syndrome, and alcoholism (Narayan, Moyes, & Wolff, 1990; www.ninds.nih.gov). Common symptoms include sensory sensitivities, hyperactivity and anxiety. Some excellent resources on autism and Asperger Syndrome include Tony Attwood's *Asperger's Syndrome: A Guide for Parents and Professionals* (1998), and the web pages for organizations such as the Autism Society of America (www.autism-society.org), the Center for the Study of Autism (www.autism.org), the National Institutes of Health (www.nih.gov), and the Mayo Foundation for Medical Education and Research (www.mayoclinic.com).

Types of Autism

Not all children or adults on the autism spectrum have all of the symptoms discussed here and are not diagnosed with the classical form of autism. Those with behavior problems such as social awkwardness who do not have language problems often are diagnosed with Asperger Syndrome. Individuals with this milder type of autism tend to function more comfortably in the community and demonstrate more typical thinking and speech patterns. Yet, both groups have difficulty with flexible problem solving, social interactions, facial recognition, and fine-motor coordination, for example.

The more severe kind of autism presents with more obvious neurological problems, which include auditory processing deficits and the inability to understand speech. Individuals with this kind of autism may not be able to hear complex speech sounds; some cannot follow simple commands. Even though a pure-tone hearing test may yield nor-

People on the autism spectrum may act very differently from each other, even if they have the same diagnosis.

mal results, the child or adult may not be able to understand speech. Hearing the consonant sounds may be especially difficult. In severe cases, the child may hear only vowels. My speech teacher helped me hear the consonants by stretching them out and enunciating them. She would hold up a cup and say, "ccccuppppp." When grownups talked fast, I could not understand them. For a long time, I thought grownups had a special "grownup" language.

A number of individuals with this form of autism also show signs of subtle seizures such as staring or "spacing out." Others experience a mixing of sensory channels. For example, sounds may come through as color or touch as a sound-like sensation (Cesaroni & Garber, 1991). Some individuals simply do not know where their body boundaries are. Many are considered low functioning and have low IQ scores. Some have developmental disabilities and a lower IQ, but others simply have serious sensory processing problems that make communication difficult.

Of course, the higher functioning the person with autism is, the more complex the job he or she can usually hold. For example, I know college professors, business owners and engineers on the autism spectrum who go to work every day and manage themselves quite well. Regardless, the outside world is usually not a welcoming place for those of us with such acute differences from the norm, primarily because our sensory and nervous systems are often pretty raw. Noises too loud and sudden, touch too strong or too soft, smells too intense, tastes too extreme, and visuals too stimulating can send us over the edge – or shut us down into withdrawal.

Yet, we are not all alike, for as mentioned earlier, autism affects people differently. Popular opinion paints those on the autism spectrum as having little emotional contact with the outside world, including not making eye contact, showing affection, smiling or laughing. But this is an overgeneralization and, like most other generalizations, is not entirely factual. It is true that many withdraw, but just like others, they respond to their environment in both positive and negative ways. When we are tired, we might feel disjointed, a bit lost. With enough sleep, you'll find us laughing with coworkers, enjoying a sunny day, or a quiet time with our family.

I know college professors, business owners and engineers on the autism spectrum who go to work every day and manage themselves quite well.

Major Challenges

The challenges people on the autism spectrum face can include all or some of the following:

▶ **Problems with social skills and developing friendships.** This occurs for a variety of reasons. Often the person on the spectrum hyper-focuses on favorite subjects, talking non-stop about them and missing social cues from others to stop. Sometimes people on the spectrum tune out others when they find themselves becoming overstimulated or anxious. Individuals may act aloof, keeping themselves apart from others as a way to manage their anxieties. As a result, they can appear unfriendly, sometimes even rude.

▶ **Difficulty in carrying on conversations.** This challenge is fairly common for people on the spectrum. Because our interests can be obscure, they may not be interesting to others. But often, that doesn't stop us from talking on and on about them.

▶ **No receptive speech.** The most severely affected individuals cannot speak, even though they may have more normal thinking patterns and emotions. Incoming speech sounds may fade in and out, or they may be a jumble of sound.

▶ **Obsession with rituals or restricted behavioral patterns.** Sameness is very important to people on the autism spectrum. Wearing the same clothing, traveling the same route to work or school each day, and eating the same foods at each meal are common. They may also practice behaviors such as rocking or hand flapping as a way to stimulate or soothe their nervous systems.

▶ **Sensory problems.** Difficulties in this area occur because an individual's neurological system is not sending and processing messages in a smooth, even manner. Smells that are too strong or textures that are too rough, for example, can upset the sensory

Often the person on the spectrum hyper-focuses on favorite subjects, talking non-stop about them and missing social cues from others to stop.

The world is a "social" place, and all sorts of problems can occur when you can't tell that people around you are upset with your behavior or uncomfortable about the topic you are discussing with them.

system to the point that an individual becomes irritated and overwhelmed.

▶ **Fine- and gross-motor difficulties.** These problems are also related to the sensory system, which fails to send the proper messages to the muscular system. As a result, the person may be uncoordinated, drop things, and even fall down easily.

▶ **Difficulty understanding others' thoughts.** This means it can be difficult for individuals on the spectrum to read social, facial, and other important behavioral cues. The world is a "social" place, and all sorts of problems can occur when you can't tell that people around you are upset with your behavior or uncomfortable about the topic you are discussing with them. I have gotten into a lot of trouble at jobs for bluntly criticizing others' work or showing up in inappropriate clothing for the workplace. It took several concerned mentors to help me figure my way through the fallout from those situations.

▶ **Tantrums.** Life can be so confusing and upsetting for people on the autism spectrum that they tantrum when they become overwhelmed. As a youngster, I would tantrum when I became frustrated with my inability to communicate verbally with my family. It is a way, although not a very effective one, to let off steam built up from an overload of anxieties and frustrations.

▶ **Theory of mind.** Often people on the autism spectrum have a difficult time understanding that others may have different ideas on subjects or may disagree with them about a subject. For example, I once wrote a letter to the president of the company at which I was working that essentially said his employees had done a horrible job of installing some equipment. He was furious and horribly embarrassed, of course, which I could not understand at the time. Once again, my mentors stepped in to help me understand the situation – and save my job!

▶ **Anxiety.** For many of us, anxiety is a major problem, especially when dealing with a new situation. Our nervous systems seem rawer than those of others who are not on the autism spectrum. Sometimes using more than one sensory channel will cause us to shut down. For instance, some may not understand speech if they are focusing on the speaker's facial expression. Others may not notice physical sensations if they are listening to somebody talk at the same time. This overload can lead to anxiety, sometimes even panic attacks.

▶ **Depression and other emotional problems.** Life can be so difficult and confusing for people with autism spectrum disorders that they end up suffering from depression and other serious emotional problems. Just as these disorders can wreak havoc in nonautistic individuals' lives, they can have a devastating effect on those with ASD. Thankfully, there are now wonderful medications and other treatments that can help alleviate some of the effects of these problems.

In the next chapter we will look at how to manage some of the most salient characteristics of autism spectrum disorders in the workplace to help you secure and maintain a job.

> Life can be so confusing and upsetting for people on the autism spectrum that they tantrum when they become overwhelmed.

CHAPTER 2

Easing into the Workplace

*I*n order for many on the autism spectrum to join the workforce, their sensory sensitivities must be "smoothed," communication skills built, and anxiety reduced through treatment and, sometimes, medication. In the following, we will take a closer look at the major sensory issues affecting survival in the world of work and ways to cope.

The Sensory System

The sensory system helps the body maintain equilibrium in a very complex world. It brings vital information from the outside world into our inside world. In a typical working nervous system, that information flows smoothly through the nervous system into the brain, which acts as a traffic cop of sorts. That is, the brain tells the appropriate body part to move, stop doing what it is doing, slow down, and so on.

A person with ASD has trouble processing information from the outside world because sensory problems literally make it difficult to understand what is being seen, heard, and touched. It's as if there is no volume control in the incoming sensory stimuli. Sounds that would not bother neurotypical persons can make you feel as if you were inside the speakers at a booming rock concert. Sounds such as those coming from a smoke alarm hurt like a dentist drill hitting a nerve. That is, in most individuals with autism spectrum disorders the sensory system does not work in an organized fashion. Instead,

Sensory problems literally make it difficult to understand what is being seen, heard, and touched.

sensory messages may course through the nervous system, bombarding the brain with an overload of information, or too little information, which can be just as bad. It's as if there are detours everywhere, sending the nerve signals off on tangents, down dead ends and through unmarked roads. The result can be a lot of anxiety, confusion and subsequently upset or irritable behaviors for both children and adults with autism. Upset behavior for adults translates into irritability, withdrawal, anxiety, confusion, and even anger.

A simple way to determine if a child or adult has severe sensory problems is to watch his/her reaction at a busy supermarket. If every trip results in a screaming tantrum, it is safe to conclude that sensory overload is the cause. Sensory problems on the autism spectrum are very variable from person to person. Some have mild problems; for others, they are severe. In some individuals, the problems are mainly auditory and, in others, mainly visual. Nonverbal persons may experience severe sensory scrambling in both the visual and auditory systems. They may "hear" something, but perceive the communication visually, or they may be "seeing" something and experience it auditorally. Their problems are in the brain; the eyes and ears are usually normal.

Although all human beings suffer from the above symptoms at times, people on the autism spectrum generally suffer from them more often and intensely. Luckily, there are ways to manage so they occur less frequently – and rarely at work. After a general overview, we will examine the following sensory sensitivities: auditory, visual, tactile, and smell.

Sensory Problems on the Job

Individuals with severe sensory problems often have difficulty with the work environment. A talented computer programmer I know quit his job because he could not stand the noise in the office. Making the workplace tolerable for individuals with severe sensory oversensitivity usually requires some simple modifications in the environment along with the person with autism spectrum disorders trying to reduce his or her sensitivities. Success is more likely if both of these approaches are used.

Let me use myself as an example. Loud high-pitched noises can startle me and make me lose my train of thought. I teach on the college level, but I could never teach a class of

Making the workplace tolerable for individuals with severe sensory oversensitivity usually requires some simple modifications in the environment along with the person with autism spectrum disorders trying to reduce his or her sensitivities.

very young children because their high-pitched voices and quick movements would make me crazy. My fine-motor skills aren't too bad, but I know others on the spectrum who can barely write, and, for sure, should never be near a hammer and nails. If I'm in a crowd where everyone is talking at once, I won't be able to hear the person with whom I am conversing – or the rest of the people, for that matter. If their voices are of different pitches, I'll tune everyone out even faster.

Smells don't bother me too much, but they are a problem for many on the spectrum. Can you imagine being sensitive to smell and having to sit next to a woman wearing strong perfume at a meeting? You wouldn't hear or see any of the meeting because all you could think of was escaping the smell. Then, once you did, you would feel so sick you couldn't concentrate for the rest of the day.

For reasons like these, it is easy to see how the average American workplace could cause sensory overload for some of us on the autism spectrum – unless we go to work prepared to modulate our senses, and, of course, our reactions to stress. See Table 2.1 for some ways to manage these sensitivities.

Sound Sensitivity

For many on the spectrum, sound sensitivity is a huge issue. It certainly is for me. When I was a child, my hearing was so sensitive that it was as though my ears were a microphone amplifying the sounds around me. My hearing tests as normal, but I can't modulate incoming sounds. So I have two choices: (a) turn on my hearing and be deluged with sound or (b) shut off my hearing. Needless to say, neither of these options works in all situations, especially in the workplace. As an adult, my sound sensitivity problems have become less severe, but many individuals have severe sound sensitivity problems for their whole life.

The typical workplace is full of different kinds of sounds and pitches that can be distracting and uncomfortable, sometimes downright painful: fire alarms, squealing microphone feedback, chairs scraping the floor, along with all the coworkers' and others' voices. For example, I can't hear on the phone in a busy airport or a noisy office due to the distractions, and continuous sounds such as a vent are particularly annoying.

Table 2.1: Sensory Sensitivities and How to Manage Them

Sensory Sensitivity	Problem	Solution
Auditory Sensitivity	Difficulty modulating sounds	▶ Wear earplugs ▶ Listen to music through headphones ▶ Turn down telephone ringer volume ▶ Have "white noise" such as a fan's whirring, indoor fountain or environmental music in background ▶ Record offending sound and gradually get used to it through exposure
	Difficulty understanding spoken messages and other sounds	▶ Write down oral messages as you hear them ▶ Rely on written communications ▶ Chew gum to help auditory focus
Visual Sensitivity	Fluorescent lighting's buzzing and flickering is irritating, distracting	▶ Wear a hat with a brim ▶ Put desk near window for better natural lighting ▶ Use 100-watt incandescent bulb in light fixture ▶ Wear tinted glasses ▶ Use laptop computer (less flickering on screen) or flat-screen desktop computer (also less flickering)
	Can't find papers, objects (not processing visual information fast enough)	▶ Provide visual structure through color coding of files ▶ Keep the files of current projects on or near your desk for easy reach. Keep old files in a file cabinet away from the desk so they don't clutter the area
	Harsh contrast between light is distracting	▶ Copy reading materials on tan, dark gray, light blue or green paper to reduce contrast. Use colored overlays over reading material or tinted glasses

Sensory Sensitivity	Problem	Solution
Visual Sensitivity	Seeing people walk by is distracting	▶ Move work area out of heavily trafficked areas ▶ Have desk face wall instead of hallway
Tactile Sensitivity	Light touch is irritating and distracting	▶ Wear soft clothing without tags ▶ Buy clothes from thrift store because they are usually softer than new ones
Smell Sensitivity	Smells nauseate or make dizzy	▶ Chew peppermint or cinnamon gum to cover up smell or have scent diffuser with green apple scent for focus, vanilla or lavender for calming, and peppermint for energizing nervous system ▶ Ask nearby workmates not to wear strong perfume
Anger or Anxiety at Work	Lose temper easily	▶ Practice de-stressing techniques (for example, deep breathing, calming ritual after work) ▶ Eat crunchy or chewy foods to calm the nervous system and sour or strong foods such as lemon drops or peppermint to energize nervous system ▶ Get aerobic exercise ▶ Leave confrontations before they escalate ▶ Problem solve with supervisor/colleagues ▶ Use diplomacy ▶ Pay attention to others' body language ▶ Practice relaxation techniques such as deep breathing, visualization ▶ Cultivate allies at work ▶ Use medication, if appropriate ▶ Avoid discussing controversial subjects ▶ Switch from anger to crying

From S. Banker. (2003). Personal interview. Children's Therapy Group, Overland Park, Kansas.

Before they even hear the dreaded sound, many children on the autism spectrum misbehave if they fear a noise is going to occur; adults, on the other hand, may become withdrawn or irritable when they are apprehensive about noises. They appear to go into the "fright, fight or flight" mode.

▶ **What to Do.** Wearing earplugs can help mute the distracting and loud noises at work, but they should never be worn all day to prevent the sensory system from "over-accommodating" for the diluted sounds. That is, wearing earplugs all the time may make sound sensitivity worse. Listening to music through headphones can block out unwanted sounds and help maintain a relaxed attitude. Occupational therapist Sarah Banker, OTR/L, (2003) suggests covering up irritating sounds with a relaxing sound such as "white noise" or water from a small indoor fountain. For some, a fan's whirring is calming, a kind of white noise itself. Another solution would be to play environmental music at work, if permitted and appropriate. Some mobile phones have ringers that are difficult to tolerate. Changing the ring on the phones in the vicinity may help.

Persons with auditory-processing problems, that is, an inability to properly understand, comprehend and process information that is heard, usually have difficulty understanding spoken messages as well as responding to other sounds at the same time. Banker (2003) suggests they rely on written messages for most of their communication, but also write down oral messages as they listen to them. In addition, she says, chewing gum may also help concentration and makes remembering messages easier.

Another method that may help reduce sound sensitivity is making a recording of the offending sound. The person plays the recording back at a very low volume and gradually increases it. The person must control both the volume and the length of time the sound is played.

Before they even hear the dreaded sound, many children on the autism spectrum misbehave if they fear a noise is going to occur; adults, on the other hand, may become withdrawn or irritable when they are apprehensive about noises.

Visual Sensitivity

Probably the biggest visual problem in the workplace is fluorescent lighting. Not only does the buzzing sound bother many
on the autism spectrum, so does the light's constant flickering,
which otherwise goes unnoticed by most. Researchers have
reported that fluorescent lighting can increase the repetitive
behavior of some children on the autism spectrum (Coleman,
Frankel, Ritvo, & Freeman, 1976).

▶ **What to Do.** Fluorescent lights drive some individuals
with autism spectrum disorders crazy because they
can see the flickering that turns on and off at 60
cycles per second. It makes the office look like a
disco, not a particularly workplace-like environment,
and definitely distracting. If you can't dismantle the
lights, wearing a hat with a brim can solve some of
the problem. A lamp with a 100-watt incandescent
bulb is another way to reduce flickering in the work
area. Finally, placing the desk or workstation near a
window to get natural light will also help, if possible.

Irlen tinted lenses have helped some people with visual
sensitivity. Developed by Helen Irlen, these lenses have
especially helped people with problems perceiving their
surroundings and difficulty reading (Irlen, 1991). These
glasses help their wearers feel more relaxed, be less
bothered by bright lighting, and be less distracted by
perceptual distortions that can throw off their motor
coordination. A person must choose the color lens that
works best for him or her. Another option is to choose
from the different tinted glasses in pale colors available
at local sunglass stores. I find the pale pinks, purples
and browns are helpful. Even though many claim that
colored lenses help them, Irlen lenses are generally considered a controversial therapy as their effectiveness has
not been empirically validated.

Occupational therapist Banker (2003) suggests people
wear dark-tinted glasses, adjust the brightness of
their computer screens or, better yet, replace TV-type
monitors with flat-screen monitors, which do not

Probably the biggest visual problem in the workplace is fluorescent lighting.

flicker as much. Sometimes laptops work better than a desktop flat panel because some flat-panel displays have fluorescent lights inside. I know several students whose academic careers were saved by laptop computers that had a screen that did not flicker.

For some on the autism spectrum, it's the ability to see too much that causes the overstimulation. In those cases, it helps to arrange the work area so that the person is not near or facing a high-traffic area. Placing the person's desk against a wall to block the distraction may also help. Fortunately, many newer offices have higher cubicle walls that help block annoying distractions.

For some, visual sensitivity can mean not being able to find what they are looking for. They are not processing visual information quickly enough and literally cannot find the one item they need at a given moment. Reading may be easier if reading materials are printed on tan, gray, light blue and light green paper, which reduces contrast. Colored transparent overlays are also helpful to many people. Experiment with different colors to see what works best.

Tactile (Touch) Sensitivities

One of the first ways parents suspect that something is "wrong" with their child with autism spectrum disorders usually involves tactile sensitivities. Many are diagnosed around age two or three because their parents are concerned about their toddler's inability to connect with them. For example, parents may hug and don't get hugged back. When my mother would hug me, I stiffened and pulled away because the physical sensation was too much for me to handle. As much as I craved being held, I avoided touch.

This tactile defensiveness is a problem in the workplace as well. If, for example, a colleague walks by and accidentally brushes the individual, that kind of light touch can make people with tactile defensiveness jump out of their skin or start a fight, guaranteed to get them fired. Scratchy woolen clothes, shirt tags, sock strings – all can distract the person on the autism spectrum so much that he or she can't work effectively.

One of the first ways parents suspect that something is "wrong" with their child with autism spectrum disorders usually involves tactile sensitivities.

▶ **What to Do.** Tactile defensiveness is one of the easiest problems to handle in the workplace. For one, Banker (2003) suggests, make sure clothing is comfortable, which may mean cutting out tags in shirts, wearing underwear inside out, and choosing clothes made from soft material. Clothes that have been washed many times are often more comfortable than new, stiffer clothes. Some people have discovered that clothes obtained from a thrift store may be softer and more comfortable for the same reason.

If the workplace is large with lots of people around, persons with tactile defensiveness should try to have their workstation on the perimeter so they can avoid jostling and bumping. They also want to keep themselves regulated, Banker says, by practicing relaxation techniques: deep breathing, soft music, if appropriate, and a de-stressing ritual after work. Eating crunchy or chewy foods is also a way to calm the nervous system. For those who need a burst of energy or focus, eating sour foods such as lemon drops or strong-tasting peppermints can provide a boost.

Smell Sensitivities

Smells can be quite distracting to people on the autism spectrum and, although this sensitivity is not as common as some of the others discussed here, it can still make life difficult. Imagine becoming nauseated or dizzy every time the person in the next workstation used hand lotion, ate a garlicky dish for lunch, or simply had a case of bad breath. The smell of perfume is obnoxious for some; others may not be bothered by it at all.

▶ **What to Do.** One easy way to reduce the discomforts of smell is to chew gum, for the mint or cinnamon smell of the gum will float around the nose level covering up other unpleasant smells, Banker (2003) says. Another approach is to use some of the many products on the market specifically designed to cover up odors. For example, Banker points out that green apple scent is good for focus, vanilla and

Tactile defensiveness is a problem in the workplace as well.

lavender are calming, and peppermint is energizing. Candles also work well to diffuse troubling smells but since they are forbidden in most workplaces for safety reasons, using a scent diffuser is best. In some cases, it may be possible to ask a coworker to not wear the offending perfume at work.

Other Tools

Listening Therapies

One treatment for helping some people with sensory problems is "listening therapy," which relies on specially modulated music to desensitize the sensory system. However, it does not work for everyone. This is one of the challenges when dealing with autism – a treatment that works for one does not necessarily work for another.

Some of the benefits of listening programs (auditory training) for some individuals are:

▶ Reducing sound sensitivity

▶ Improving receptive and expressive language

▶ Reducing stress from sensory overload

The Alert Program

The Alert Program teaches people of all ages how to regulate their sensory systems using techniques developed over the years by occupational therapists. The Alert Program was created by occupational therapists Mary Sue Williams and Sherry Shellenberger, whose 1996 book, *How Does Your Engine Run? A Leader's Guide to the Alert Program for Self-Regulation*, describes in detail the strategies for changing or maintaining states of alertness as well as the underlying theory of sensory integration (www.alertprogram.com). The program teaches participants first how to track their energy level and then how to slow themselves down or speed themselves up, depending on the situation. For example, if you need to calm down and focus your thoughts, you could stretch your arms against a wall and do a few quick arm

> One treatment for helping some people with sensory problems is "listening therapy," which relies on specially modulated music to desensitize the sensory system.

push-ups. Right before you take a test, reach out with your arms across your body to energize both sides of the brain.

Controlling Anger

A major problem for many people on the spectrum is modulating emotions. Because of their sensory processing problems, they often feel frustrated and angry. With so much stimulation coming at them, they may feel as if their environment is out of their control. Some lose their cool and lash out, whereas others become anxious and shut down. Either way, the emotional ups and downs can be a major problem for the individual with ASD as well as for those around.

Losing your temper at work is threatening and frightening to your colleagues. Shutting down and not communicating is also a problem when you are in the workplace. Either one won't be tolerated for long, especially in these tense and violence-wary times. One of the major reasons people get fired from a job is their failure to get along with others. So knowing what to do when you are finding yourself losing control is a major part of your life education.

Anger outbursts won't be tolerated, either in school or the workplace. In short, if you hit somebody or throw a computer, you are fired. After getting in several fistfights in high school when other students teased me, I learned to control my anger by switching my emotion from anger to crying. I had to learn to control my temper because I had been kicked out of a large high school for throwing a book at a girl who teased me. Similarly, at the boarding school I attended, horse back riding was taken away after I got into a fistfight.

After that I switched my emotion from anger to crying. As a result, when I had a problem with a coworker, I hid in the cattle corral and cried. Crying is tolerated at work – intense anger is not. I learned that anger for me was like a snarling lion in a cage. It is too dangerous to open the cage door even one inch because if the lion shoves the door open, I cannot control him.

I have worked at many meat plants on new equipment installation. It is normal during installations of equipment for things to go wrong and to lose production time. Plant managers who have never experienced a major equipment installation often think the new equipment will work per-

> A major problem for many people on the spectrum is modulating emotions.

One of
the major
reasons
people get
fired from a
job is their
failure to get
along with
others.
So knowing
what to do
when you
are finding
yourself
losing control
is a major
part of
your life
education.

fectly in the first five minutes. On several projects, when things went wrong, the plant manager screamed at me. To prevent losing my temper, I looked at him as if he were a two-year-old having a tantrum because he thinks I broke his toy. I used to call this the tantrum phrase of new equipment startups. In these instances, I calmly took the manager by the hand and led him back to the conference room and explained to him that his plant was not broken and that some loss of production was normal.

I then told him about other equipment startups that went really badly and reassured him that the startup in his plant was going well compared to other plants. There were other times I was yelled at while operating a new piece of equipment and just kept operating the equipment without responding. After the manager left, I went out into the cattle corrals and cried.

Throughout my career, I have never had an anger incident that would have jeopardized my job as I deliberately developed a way to deal with difficult situations that I knew would upset me.

▶ **What to Do.** You must develop strategies for controlling anger if you want to keep your job. It is easier for a girl to switch to crying than for a guy, but crying is still preferable to getting fired, no matter who you are. There may be coworkers who deliberately try to provoke you. If that happens, this may be a good time to talk to your boss and possibly switch your workstation or transfer to another department or area. Another tactic is to cultivate powerful allies who can help you deal with a mean coworker.

As a general rule, avoid discussing controversial religious, political or sexual topics at work. Opinionated views on these subjects can make coworkers dislike you. There are times when you have to politely say that you are feeling stressed and have to go outside to calm down. Always leave the confrontation before it escalates. Also, you may have an easier time controlling anger if you get plenty of aerobic exercise. Vigorous exercise calms down the nervous system and helps you focus. In addition to medication, as discussed below, meditation and relaxation exercises can help control anger and other strong emotions. Both meditation and relaxation exercises can be done at work. Find an empty room or a bench outside where you can go when you feel you are going to lose your temper. If you do blow up, you must go outside and get away from your coworkers immediately, before you end up doing something violent or saying something you will regret later. In today's world, there is zero tolerance for violent behavior.

Medication

Medication is one of the tools used increasingly to modulate sensory system problems and control depression and anxiety. In recent years we have learned much about the brain and a host of medications have been developed that can help people on the autism spectrum to lead more typical and productive lives. Managing one's challenges through medication is a decision that needs to be taken very seriously. When considering this option, start out by finding a competent doctor. Ask for recommendations from people you know in support groups, for example.

Medication has worked well for me for many years. As I wrote in *Thinking in Pictures* (1995), I became very anxious when I entered puberty, and those anxieties intensified as I grew older. Others may have a few problems at puberty and then calm down and never need medication to deal with their problems. My anxiety made me feel as if I were in a constant state of "stage fright." I lived with this anxiety disorder until I turned 34 and went through eye surgery, which intensified my anxieties even more. I read as much as I could about possible biochemical answers to my problem before asking my doctor to prescribe an antidepressant that researchers had discovered decreased anxieties.

Within two days, I could feel a difference. I have come to realize that without the antidepressant, my body is in a constant state of physiological vigilance, ready to flee nonexistent predators. That is common for many on the autism spectrum, due to our sensitive nervous systems. But it is also true for many nonautistic individuals who suffer from depression and anxiety, and whose nervous systems are biologically prepared for flight.

As a general rule, avoid discussing controversial religious, political or sexual topics at work.

After three years I switched to another antidepressant, which was in the same family of medications but has had fewer side effects for me. Today there are even more choices of medications for people on the autism spectrum with generally even fewer side effects such as dry mouth and constipation. The newest SSRIs (Selective Serotonin Reuptake Inhibitors) are preferred.

Although medication can be a lifesaver for many on the autism spectrum, the wrong dose – or the wrong medication – can wreak havoc. I have heard many horror stories of how giving the wrong drug to someone on the autism spectrum with epilepsy can cause grand mal seizures, or how too high a dose of antidepressant sent the person into a rage.

▶ **What to Do.** The general rule for medications for those on the spectrum is to start off low and stay low. According to Dr. Paul Hardy, an autism specialist in Boston, and Dr. John Ratey, a psychiatrist with the Harvard Medical School, people with autism often require lower doses of antidepressants than nonautistic people due to abnormal development of serotonin systems in the brain (Hardy, 1989; Ratey et al., 1987). Some only need one fourth to one third of the normal dose. Too high of a dose causes agitation, aggression, excitability, with insomnia being the first symptom if the dose is not correct. When these symptoms occur, the antidepressant must either be stopped or the dose must be reduced (Hardy, 1989; Ratey et al., 1987). Such decisions should always be made in consultation with one's physician.

People on the autism spectrum sometimes use Risperidal to control rage and aggression. Again, Dr. Joe Huggins, an autism specialist in Canada, found that the dose must be kept very low for people on the spectrum (Huggins, 1995). Sometimes a combination of medication, diet, and a sensory treatment is more effective than any one treatment alone.

Donna Williams, the author of *Nobody Nowhere and Somebody Somewhere* (1992), described very severe visual problems. In addition, her sound sensitivity

Although medication can be a lifesaver for many on the autism spectrum, the wrong dose – or the wrong medication – can wreak havoc.

problems were so severe that she could not even tolerate clapping at a conference. Today a combination of a
casein- and gluten-free diet, Irlen lenses and a tiny
dose of Risperidal makes it possible for her to tolerate
being in a large convention hall. When I saw her at a
convention recently, she was the new Donna. The
combination of conventional medicines and alterna-
tive treatments was very successful. For Donna,
Risperidal helped reduce her sensory problems, but it
was also essential for her to continue her special diet.

Be open-minded and try different things. Some are
helped by vitamin supplements such as B6 and mag-
nesium and dimethyglycine (DMG). Information on
the DAN (Defeat Autism Now) protocol can be
obtained from Dr. Bernard Rimland's Autism
Research Institute in San Diego (www.autism.com).
It contains information on diets and supplements
that may be helpful.

Medication should never be considered the only
tool for helping a person on the autism spectrum
lead a fruitful life. Teaching and coaching life skills
is a critical part of the treatment. Exercise, too, is
extremely helpful in calming a person down. For
me, exercise has helped reduce my anxiety and
improve my sleep. Not only does it tone the body,
it also produces endorphins – brain chemicals that
help you feel good and stay focused.

Whatever you decide about medication, make sure you
read about the different types and work with an experienced doctor in determining which type would be best
for you. Sometimes you will have to try several to find
the one that works the best. Don't be put off by that, for
that is part of making a good decision about your life.

Medication should never be considered the only tool for helping a person on the autism spectrum lead a fruitful life. Teaching and coaching life skills is a critical part of the treatment.

Social Skills for the Workplace

Employers will tell you that one of the major reasons people don't do well in the workplace is that they can't get along with their colleagues. This is a big problem for everybody but can be devastating for those of us with autism spectrum disorders. To keep the workplace running smoothly, people have to get along. There's no way around it, so figuring out how to do so is an important part of your education. Oddly enough, work-related social problems are often less severe for people on the spectrum who have more obvious disabilities, such as no speech. Once other employees understand autism, they are often very helpful. It is the people who are closer to being typical who have the worst problems with office politics and jealousy.

Getting in trouble socially is a big problem for individuals on the autism spectrum. Many people with autism are socially naïve, expecting everybody to be honest and kind. It can be a rude awakening to discover there are some people in the world who might exploit us. Ideally, your employer should let your fellow employees know about your autism, so they can be more understanding and forgiving of some of our more eccentric traits – our fixation on certain subjects and sometimes odd dress. Of course, that assumes you have disclosed your disability. That brings up a whole other issue: whether or not to self-disclose. In many technical fields, people with Asperger Syndrome or autistic-like behaviors are very common, and it may be better to avoid disclosure. In fields that require more social skills, disclosure may be advisable (see the Appendix for more information).

Some of autistic individuals' strengths can be a problem on the job. For example, our ability to focus intently can mean it's difficult for us to make transitions. That kind of focus can also make it difficult to supervise others, especially if there is a lot of customer and colleague contact. I know one fellow who had worked successfully for a number of years at an architectural firm only to lose his job after he was promoted to a position that required a great deal of customer contact. Also, during conferences I have talked to highly skilled people on the autism spectrum who lost good jobs when they were promoted into management.

In response to this problem, some engineering firms are changing their policies to allow their good "techies" to

Employers will tell you that one of the major reasons people don't do well in the workplace is that they can't get along with their colleagues.

advance along a "techie" track and not ruin them by making them managers. Related to the same issue, Massachusetts Institute for Technology (MIT), the famous engineering university, now offers social skills classes. Many engineers have autistic or Asperger traits. A study by Simon Baron-Cohen (2000) in England indicated that there were twice as many engineers in the family histories of people on the autism spectrum. That is certainly true for me. My grandfather was an MIT-trained engineer who was a co-inventor of the automatic pilot for airplanes.

Getting Along with Others

Probably the most important social skill to learn is knowing how to read coworkers' emotions and social cues. I have heard a number of stories of people on the autism spectrum losing their jobs because they did not recognize that their coworkers either did not like them or were jealous of their talents.

One person was fired because his employer discovered pornography on his computer. The guy was innocent; presumably, a jealous or angry coworker planted the offensive materials. In other cases, I have had unhappy employees break equipment I had just installed in my clients' livestock facilities. In less extreme situations, you simply have to learn to deal with the ups and downs of your coworkers' lives, some of whom would like to spend way too much time describing their personal problems. You need to share some of those life experiences with each other, but too much of it makes the workplace become a tense, unhappy place.

▶ **What to Do.** When I begin work with a new client, I pay attention to the body language of the employees on whose "turf" I'll be treading. Look for the people at meetings who sit with their arms crossed, are particularly silent, or act unfriendly toward you. In my line of work, it's usually not the plant manager or superintendent or hourly worker who are jealous; it's more often the head maintenance person or engineer, who does a job similar to mine who acts in a passive-aggressive manner. You might find this person moving very slowly while working on your project with you, or perhaps she simply refuses to

Our ability to focus intently can mean it's difficult for us to make transitions at work. That kind of focus can also make it difficult to supervise others, especially if there is a lot of customer and colleague contact.

show up to help at a crucial time in the installation. Whatever the situation, there are always a million ways to mess up the job.

What can you do about this? Make a point of getting to know those people in order to defuse their anger or concern about their job. Ask for their opinion and bring them into the work you are doing as much as possible. Talk with them about their family, get to know their life and share your own experiences with them. They may feel threatened because an outsider has been hired to do what they may consider "their job." If that does not help, talk with your supervisor about the problem.

Knowing how to "talk" with coworkers, clients and customers is also key to staying on the job.

Knowing how to "talk" with coworkers, clients and customers is also key to staying on the job. Tom McKean, author of *Soon Will Come the Light* (1994), told about an experience he had with a computer programming professor who flunked him for finding a better way of writing a program. Tom would walk up to the board and erase and correct his professor's example. I'm sure Tom's direct manner and speech are what caused the problem. I'm just as sure, however, that a more creative professor could have found a way to incorporate Tom's criticisms into the class discussion. Knowing how to disagree with those in command is an important lesson to be learned.

Early in my career, when I was working with a large feedlot construction company, I sold a contract to a meat-packing plant to design and build a new cattle ramp. During construction, I tactlessly criticized some workmen's sloppy welding. The plant engineer pulled me aside and advised me to apologize before a small problem turned into a major one. I went to the cafeteria and apologized to the staff and in the process learned a great lesson about how to talk about problems with others.

If you see a problem occurring on the job, don't attack the person or his work. Instead, engage the employee in a conversation about the job. If you can get him talking about what he is doing, he might notice the mistakes he is making and rectify them.

But I didn't entirely learn the lesson, for a year later I got into a hassle with the president of the company, to whom I had written a letter criticizing the sloppy installation of some equipment at another plant. The letter embarrassed the company president because it made him look as if he ran a sloppy organization. This time it was the plant manager who bailed me out. He turned out to be one of my most important workplace mentors.

One of the greatest lessons I learned from this manager was that talent earns respect. When I first arrived at the plant, I was literally a pain. I talked way too much, probably drove him crazy, but he tolerated me because I was able to come up with some pretty clever ways to solve problems, such as using plastic milk hoses to pad gate edges and prevent the livestock from bruising.

If you are talented, you can often get away with being eccentric at work, but you usually can't get away with poor grooming – a very important part of social skills. To be out among others, you have to fit in as much as possible, and that includes the way you groom yourself. You don't have to look like everyone else, but you must not be a slob. At one of my first jobs, the construction manager, another one of my mentors, got his department secretaries to take me shopping for clothes. He was very blunt about what I had to do socially to be successful at the company, including wearing deodorant. I did not like him talking to me like that at the time, but later I realized that he had done me a huge favor.

Having mentors is an excellent way to learn the social rules of the workplace. Thanks to them and just plain experience, I have grown more tactful and diplomatic over the years. I have learned to never go

Having mentors is an excellent way to learn the social rules of the workplace.

over the head of the person who hired me unless I have his or her permission. The first lesson I had to learn was that I could not tell other people that they were stupid. I know several people on the autism spectrum who were fired because they told their boss that he was stupid.

It is our tendency to pinpoint the negative, to find the faults because they upset our sense of order. In general, look for the good things your colleagues and boss are doing on the job. That way when there are problems, you can balance them out with the positive. On one job, the plant engineer had installed the hydraulics wrong, and, as a result, we had to tear it out and rebuild it. I helped smooth his rumpled feathers by complimenting him on his beautiful electric panels. His electrical work deserved a compliment.

Learn as much diplomacy as you can before you enter the work world. Observe others, how they get along with each other. Read about talented people to find out how they got along in the world. For myself, I learned about diplomacy by reading about international negotiations and using them as models. In many situations, I just avoid the people who would cause trouble. I can usually tell who they are by their body language and facial expressions. They sit stiffly, with their arms folded and do not change their facial expressions.

Recently, a woman with autism made the following reply to my advice: "Honesty is the best way." I told her that you can still be honest without giving your opinion about everything. I told her that you were hired to do a job, not criticize the boss or your coworkers. If you have to correct somebody's mistake, say something like, "If you do it this way, it will work better."

Other advice includes refraining from gossiping and never writing e-mail containing personal information that is critical of coworkers or your boss. Never write nasty e-mails about the boss or coworkers you do not like. Many people have been fired due to inappropriate things they write in e-mail. If you want to have a private discussion with one of your coworkers about a problem in the office, do not use e-mail. Go out for lunch or sit in a park. When you delete e-mail, it doesn't go away. The boss can retrieve it off the server. At one company an employee was fired because he wrote an e-mail that said that when his boss got mad, his face looked like a "putrid, quivering pumpkin."

Another thing that can get you into trouble is gossiping about other employees. Don't do it. I talked to one lady who was a good employee but got into trouble by talking about sensitive subjects at work. Unless a person is a very close friend, it is best to avoid topics such as sex, religion and politics. Much safer subjects are sports, movies, hobbies, work-related conversation, the weather and what you did on the weekend. Extreme views on religion or politics can really turn off coworkers.

Problems with the Boss

A change of boss can cause problems for anybody – with or without autism spectrum disorders. I have met several people on the autism spectrum who had stable employment until a boss who appreciated their talents left the company. When they got a new boss, their lives became miserable, and some even lost their jobs. Tyrants who get into power make life miserable for everybody. During a 30-year consulting career, I have worked on long complex projects with about 50 companies. I have seen some very good bosses but also some bad bosses who not only made their employees' lives miserable but also did great damage to their companies.

There are two types of bad bosses. The first type is terrible for everybody. The second type may get along with the "neurotypical" people, but does not like the "weird" Asperger person. I had a problem with the second type when the magazine I worked for got a new manager. Jim, the new manager, thought I was weird and wanted to get rid of me. I was too socially inept to know what was going on, but my friend Sue in the graphics department cautioned me and subsequently

> **Never write nasty e-mails about the boss or coworkers you do not like.**

helped me assemble a portfolio of articles I had written. When Jim saw the portfolio, he recognized the value of my work and, instead of firing me, he gave me a raise.

Other situations do not work out as well. There are some people who will never get along. If you work for a large corporation or a government agency, you may be able to get transferred if you are in a situation where you do not get along with somebody, but if you work for a small company you are in trouble unless you become friendly with your colleagues and gain their support.

In some situations employees on and off the autism spectrum have no choice but to learn to work with a difficult boss. This does not lead to productive employees, but people tolerate it when jobs are scarce and they need a paycheck. The workplace is just like any other organization in your life: There is good and there is bad, and you just have to take both.

> In some situations employees on and off the autism spectrum have no choice but to learn to work with a difficult boss.

Organizational Skills at Work

Being organized at work is difficult for most people. We don't do a good job of teaching our children these very important skills. For someone on the autism spectrum, having strong organizational skills is an absolute must. They make work better, smoother, and more fulfilling. In some cases, they can mean the difference between keeping a job and losing it.

The Big Picture

To be successful on the job, everyone, autistic and nonautistic alike, needs a plan and a daily structure. There are lots of books written about this subject, so this discussion will be short.

To start off, people need to keep in mind what's important to them in life. That sounds like a huge process, but it doesn't have to be. In his book *Seven Habits of Highly Effective People* (1990), Stephen Covey advises people to write a personal mission statement that will govern how they make choices. People start this process, Covey writes, by asking what they want the different people in their lives – family, friends, neighbors, clients and colleagues – to say about them at their funerals. That is, what they want to be remembered for. For most of us, it's something nice: How kind we are to others, how great we are at certain tasks, and so on.

For example, perhaps it's important for you to become an excellent photographer, to learn as much as you can about taking memorable pictures and having them exhibited in art galleries in your home town. This goal would then become an overriding focus in your life, one you would support daily by selecting goals that would help you achieve that purpose. In other words, every step you take, every choice you make, must support that goal in your life.

Role	**Goal**
Photographer	1. Enroll in university class
	2. Practice shooting 5 rolls of film
	3. Enter local photography contest
	4. Read photography trade journal
	5. Attend local photographers' meeting and make 3 new contacts

Let that be the starting point, Covey writes, for how you decide what roles are important in life. Once the roles are decided, you select the goals for each role and plug them into a weekly calendar. It's important, Covey suggests, to plan a week at a time in order to see life's big picture. However, depending on the job, you might plan even further out or less.

Day to Day. Thom Hartman, a psychologist who writes about attention deficit disorder, also suggests people write down their goals and create timelines and other plans for how to reach those goals. In his book, *Focus Your Energy: Hunting for Success in Business with Attention Deficit Disorder* (1994), Hartman suggests that people surround themselves with written reminders of their goals so they can visualize them and make them more concrete.

Hartman also recommends the following organizational strategy for prioritizing work commitments.

To keep track of schedules, you need a big calendar on which to write project dates and appointments. I cannot use any of the new fancy electronic calendars because I have to write the information out in order to remember it. Something concrete and visual works best for most of us on the spectrum. I need a calendar where I can see the

To be successful on the job, everyone, autistic and nonautistic alike, needs a plan and a daily structure.

Table 2.2: Prioritizing Work Commitments

1. Make a daily "to-do list" on a legal pad and have two boxes on the desk or work area marked "A" and "B." Label an empty desk drawer "C."

2. Mark everything on the list and every piece of work paper with either "A, B, or C." Do this daily.

3. "A's" are the things that must be done immediately. After defining them, decide the order in which you'll do them. If they are big projects, break them into one- or two-hour blocks of time, which also get marked as "A's." Any papers for "A" projects go into the "A" box.

4. "B's" are next to be done after the "A's" are all finished. Put any "B" papers into the "B" box.

5. Finally, "C's" are least important and therefore get done last. Drop any "C" papers into the "C" drawer.

6. Check your list daily and move up "B's" into "A" slots once those most important projects are completed.

Source: Hartman, T. (1994). *Focus Your Energy: Hunting for Success in Business with Attention Deficit Disorder.* New York: Pocket Books.

---

entire month. This prevents me from mixing up my schedule. It also makes it easier to look at work that will occur several days or weeks ahead.

Since sequencing is one part of organization that is especially difficult for me as a visual thinker, I have to write everything down to keep track of what I am doing. Even today I have problems remembering a sequence to operate a new piece of equipment such as a copy machine. So I have to write down all the steps in the right order. I had trouble operating the fax machine when the written directions were removed from the machine. All I need is a list of the sequence. In the same way, all the features in mobile phones baffle me. I cannot remember which buttons to push because they are not labeled. I still prefer to use an answering service where an operator reads my messages to me and I have time to write them down. I like the phone system in hotels because getting messages is simple. I just press a button labeled "message." I still have problems getting messages off my mobile phone, so I just rely on the answering service.

Being Successful at Work

It takes a lot of interventions for someone on the autism spectrum to be able to be successful at work. Parents must start teaching their children at a young age to be responsible for their belongings and carrying out tasks. As the children grow into adulthood, these lessons will stay with them and help them be more successful – and, I believe, fulfilled in their lives.

In general, a person on the autism spectrum can make a successful transition into work by following these suggestions.

1. **Make gradual transitions** – Start working for short periods while still in high school. The time spent working should gradually be lengthened. I know one mother whose 12-year-old son wants to be a veterinarian, so she takes him to their neighborhood pet store on Saturdays to volunteer for a couple of hours. She stays with him and makes sure that he interacts with customers while he learns how to care for different kinds of animals.

2. **Seek out supportive employers** – Parents and educators should help find employers who are willing to work with people on the autism spectrum. Find employers who appreciate special talents and skills, who need those talents to keep their businesses running. This requires a lot of leg work on parents' part, but the payoff is big. Often community colleges have employment centers for their students and help build relationships with area employers. Those would be good ones to contact.

3. **Find mentors** – Mentors can help you learn important social and job skills. Mentors also can motivate students to study and introduce them to an interesting job. Mentors can sometimes be found where you least expect it. A good mentor might be the next-door neighbor who works for the power company. This person could get a young person on the spectrum motivated by taking him on a tour of an electric power plant and teaching him how a power

> Find employers who appreciate special talents and skills, who need those talents to keep their businesses running.

People on the autism spectrum have to sell their skills, not themselves, which is the opposite of the way most businesses operate.

plant works, for example. One mother I know called up the local university and paid a biology graduate student to take her son out each weekend. The son and the mentor continued that relationship long after they were both grown and on their own. Schools, churches, and neighborhoods can be good sources for mentors, so can your family. Find a willing uncle or aunt, teacher or neighbor or fellow church member.

4. **Educate employers and employees** – Both employers and coworkers need to be educated about autism spectrum disorders so they can help support the individual. They also need to understand the person's limitations in terms of social interactions, so as not to push him into situations that could lose him his job.

5. **Consider freelance work** – This is a very good career option for high-functioning individuals with special talents. By working freelance, you can organize your own structure and environment the way it best suits you so as to be more successful. Freelance work also makes it easier to avoid office politics. As a private consultant, I go in and do the job, and then leave. Nevertheless, self-employment can be stressful if it is not handled correctly. There are records to keep, marketing to be done, and clients to keep happy. Make sure you are up for those tasks before deciding to go this route.

6. **Make a portfolio** – People on the autism spectrum have to sell their skills, not themselves, which is the opposite of the way most businesses operate. Because we are not the most social beings, we have to rely heavily on our talents to get work. A portfolio of work allows potential employers or clients to see first-hand the kind of work you do and base their judgment on that and not your personality, which they may find eccentric. It may also allow you to get into the job through the back door, which is how I got all my jobs. If possible, avoid the human resources department and find someone directly in the department where you want to work.

The portfolio can also help a person keep a job. For example, if a new boss finds your social behavior "strange," her opinion may change after viewing a portfolio of your work. Portfolios will not work for every job, however. In those instances, treat your resume or job application as a portfolio and describe in concrete detail the projects, duties and successes you have had on the job. Tell how your talents helped to get a client's project designed and published in less time than the client asked for. Or perhaps you were able to program a new software system that increased your client's business by 25 percent. Be specific and detailed.

7. **Make your own web page to showcase your work** – Web pages are a great way to communicate with potential employers or clients, both of whom need to see proof of your capabilities. In some cases, this works instead of, or in addition to, a portfolio.

8. **Develop skills that other people will value and need** – People thought I was weird, but ranchers need cattle handling facilities and I made myself the very best in designing them. Today there is a huge need for translators of Middle Eastern languages, for example. So if you are good at this skill, you will be hired. I have met several people on the spectrum who became experts in highly specialized fields such as making patterns for leather coats or lighting design for theater. To make up for being considered "strange," you have to make yourself better than others in a specialized skill that other people need. By the way, no matter how much you like playing video games, video game playing is a skill few employers want!

9. **Keep your career in your talent area** – The minds of people on the spectrum are specialized. You will be good at one thing and not as good at something else. For example, I am good at visual tasks and terrible at foreign languages. Therefore, for me, switching to a translation job would not be wise. A person who is an expert with numbers may be poor at graphic design. I heard a sad story of a successful budget analyst who made a disastrous switch to web page design. He had no design talent.

Both employers and coworkers need to be educated about autism spectrum disorders so they can help support the individual.

10. **Get help with financial records and other official record keeping** – Designing complex equipment is easy for me because I can visualize it, but keeping all the paperwork straight on the business end of my freelance business is a challenge for a visual thinker. As a result, I had to have other people help me set up my corporation and show me how to separate my income from expenses for doing taxes, for example. Many visual thinkers on the spectrum need a reliable person to continuously help them with paperwork and record keeping. Some of the nonvisual thinkers who are trained in accounting may find that keeping records is easy.

11. **Manage your temper, anxieties and social skills** – This point may be last on the list, but it is critical to success in the workplace. Nothing will ruin a job faster than somebody losing their cool and blasting their colleagues. If you are going to be out in the world, take care that you do all that you can to be successful in this realm, for it is a difficult area for most of us.

Finally, remember to always focus on your talents because they are what will keep you employed. You will have to prove to people you can do the job asked of you, but with some guidance from family and colleagues, your transition into the workplace will go more smoothly.

Conclusion

To ease into the workplace, you have to deal with any sensory problems you might have that could cause you trouble. There are a number of ways to do that as discussed in this chapter. Before you go to work, learn the social rules of the work world well by practicing them at home with your family. That is very important, for the workplace is a social institution. Learn as many organizational skills as you can as a young person because you will need them at work. Spend some time learning the ways of the work world and the ways you can do your best at work.

> Remember to always focus on your talents because they are what will keep you employed.

CHAPTER 3

Rules for Success on the Job

For my work as a livestock facilities designer, I get to travel around a lot and visit many different workplaces. Over the years, I have started to notice those qualities that make a workplace more open to people on the autism spectrum. Sometimes I even find people in workplaces, who, I think, might be on the spectrum. These people are successfully employed and many of them know nothing about Asperger Syndrome or autism.

Some of the jobs in which I believe I have observed undiagnosed people on the spectrum include math teacher, copier repair technician, research scientist, industrial equipment draftsman, welder, factory maintenance staff, librarian, computer programmer, computer tech support and engineer. Keep these in mind when we later look at jobs that appear best suited for the strengths of individuals on the autism spectrum.

One of the most interesting workplaces I have visited is a small electronics and machine tool firm where the employees are downright passionate about their work. On my visit, each designer stopped me on my way through the workroom to show me what he was doing on his computer. I noticed that, although they worked in a room together, their workstations allowed them some distance from each other. I also noticed that the overhead fluorescent lights had been dismantled and that each workstation had its own soft lighting – all subtle signs that the employees' sensory sensitivities had been accommodated.

Whether you work for a small, entrepreneurial firm or a large organization, you will still have to live up to your employer's expectations.

Out in the machine shop, I got the same treatment as each guy showed off his machine and walked me through all its capabilities. Where did the employer get such passionate and interested staff members? I asked. Their supervisor told me that the company hired on talent alone and that one of the "techies" had done the interviewing. At least on the machine tool side, the staff members all came from the local community college's machining program.

While I can only suspect that some of the guys were on the autism spectrum, I know that they work in a place that would be ideal for people on the spectrum. Because the company concentrated on hiring the most talented individuals, it worried less about social skills and fitting in, usually a major concern for employers. And, they allowed new staff to be hired by one of their own – a technology wizard who looked for the same kind of skill and interest in those he interviewed. New staff also skipped the human resources department, where they might have gotten stuck. This little firm was truly an oasis for those of us on the autism spectrum. Yet, these people knew nothing about autism or Asperger Syndrome.

But despite such positives, there can be downsides to working for small firms. Larger organizations may have more opportunities for training and promotions. In a recession, they may have more financial reserves, so there might be less chance of losing your job due to the poor economy. Also, they generally have better policies and procedures in place for protecting workers' rights.

But whether you work for a small, entrepreneurial firm or a large organization, you will still have to live up to your employer's expectations. And, if you are self-employed, you will have to meet your clients' and customers' expectations.

That is what this chapter is about. It is a guide to being successful on the job, no matter what kind of job you have, big or small. Parents have a lot to do with preparing their children for success in life, but this chapter goes into the workplace itself and discusses the dos and don'ts of surviving there.

In a way, that little electronics firm I mentioned above is the ideal to which we should aspire. We need to work where our talents are respected and our colleagues are tolerant of our social eccentricities. For as hard as we try, those of us on the autism spectrum will never be entirely "socially normal." We will not be able to easily blend with others, so we

> We need to work where our talents are respected and our colleagues are tolerant of our social eccentricities.

have to become so good at what we do that employers can't afford to let us go. That means you have to know what your talent is early on and then build on it.

First, this is not an ideal world, either economically or socially, so you must be prepared as much as possible for lay-offs or even firings. One way to do that is to develop a rapport with others in your business or industry by not only doing top-notch work, but also by attending professional and trade association meetings. I realize that might be easier said than done, but it is a step that might be critical to your livelihood. A goodly percentage of jobs are passed on through word of mouth, so you have to be around others in your profession to hear of them.

Another solution is to be prepared to freelance, to work for yourself. Many professions such as graphic arts design, computer repair, bookkeeping and others can be done successfully by freelancing. Chapter 7 includes information about entrepreneurship.

Second, it is important to parlay your skills and talents to industries that are staying put, not transferring their plants, offices, or functions overseas. To know which industries are most stable, you must keep up with the social and economic trends that are shaping our now-global economy. That is very important for anyone in today's workplace, but especially important for those of us considered more "dispensable" to the success of the business.

I realize this may sound like a tall order, given our global and very mobile economy. It's best to look at industries and professions that are here to stay, that don't benefit by moving away. Look at the basics in life, those jobs that take care of our daily needs – food, housing, transportation and schooling, to name a few. Look at the food industry and all its related businesses – equipment manufacturers, installers, and technicians. Then there are the repair jobs, the mechanics who fix our cars, airplanes, computers, plumbing, and electrical systems. There are the maintenance staff who repair assembly lines, the tellers who count out your money at the bank, the technician who maintains the school's heating and cooling systems, and the clerk who tracks the library's book collection.

To keep up with the general economy is fairly simple: Regularly read your local newspaper's business section to find out local as well as global news. At the public library,

> To know which industries are most stable, you must keep up with the social and economic trends that are shaping our now-global economy.

you'll be able to find a host of newspapers and business publications as well as trade and professional journals. Read them weekly, so you know what is going on and what to expect. Search the Internet to learn about interesting careers, some of which you may never have thought of. Guidance counselors should encourage parents who work in different careers to donate trade magazines to the school library. Every profession has its professional or trade magazines, ranging from banking to car washes to building construction. These magazines will enable you to learn about all types of interesting jobs.

For a detailed look at the economy, check out the following:

► *The Wall Street Journal* – My father subscribed me to this wonderful, in-depth, five-day-a-week business newspaper when I was a teenager. I still read it religiously to keep up with general business news as well as my own industry's news, but also to learn more about social protocol, networking, office behaviors, and other social rules that do not come easy for me. Some of the regular columns include "Cubicle Culture," "The Jungle," and "Your Career Matters." I strongly recommend that both guidance counselors and students in high school subscribe to *The Wall Street Journal*.

► The *Occupational Outlook Handbook* – This very thick reference comes out of the United States Department of Labor every two years and includes key information on specific professions as well as a wonderful description of the economy as a whole. You can access this in both book form and the online version to check how your particular profession is faring (www.bls.gov/oco/).

► *Fortune Magazine* and *Fortune Small Business Magazine* – Every year this business publication produces its "100 Best Companies to Work For" issue, which is a great source of information about the companies workers value most. This beginning-of-the-year issue usually describes the winning companies' corporate cultures, an excellent

Guidance counselors should encourage parents who work in different careers to donate trade magazines to the school library. Every profession has its professional or trade magazines. These magazines will enable you to learn about all types of interesting jobs.

barometer of how employers view and respect their staff members. If a company is on this list, you can bet it is more tolerant of social eccentricities.

▶ *Inc.* – This in-depth publication chronicles in great detail news and information about small, entrepreneurial businesses, which provide much of the employment in the United States. Often the more entrepreneurial a company is, the more it values talent and the less it worries about social conformity.

▶ *Trade Magazines* – Read trade magazines from different industries, many of which can be accessed on the Internet.

▶ *Trade Shows* – Visit conventions and trade shows to talk with people working in the field and learn about trends that way. While in Chicago recently, I visited the food industry's annual convention and saw all the interesting and new equipment for that field.

There are more, of course, but these are a good start on building a regular reading list. Information and talent are essentials to being employed in the 21st century, but they need to be practiced regularly to keep them fit. I can't stress enough that social skills for those of us on the spectrum will never be entirely smooth, so we have to have other things going for us. We have to be realistic about what will help us lead fruitful and good lives.

Based on some 30 years of travels down the autism spectrum, I have found that those who do the best have three things going for them:

▶ Talent that was developed over time into skills that can be used in a career.

▶ Mentors who helped guide them through their often confusing teen and young adult years, and who helped them get involved in interesting careers.

▶ Proper medication to help manage their sensory,

Often the more entrepreneurial a company is, the more it values talent and the less it worries about social conformity.

anxiety or depression problems. (Note: Some individuals do not need or do not choose to use medication.)

In addition, the most successful work hard, are on time, constantly upgrade their skills, and try hard to get along with their colleagues. You may not like your colleagues or agree with them, but you must be respectful of them and tolerant of their differences. In other words, you treat people the way you want to be treated.

The following six rules are the basics for being successful on the job, no matter what the job.

Rule #1: Know your strengths and your limits.

Being successful at work is like anything else: pay careful attention to what works best for you, how you like to spend your time, and what activities make you feel particularly creative and strong. That is not all there is to it, of course, but that's a lot of it.

Work, for the most part, is a social activity, even if you work alone. Sooner or later, you're going to have to deliver your work to a client or employer, and it's best if you learn how to work with others – to a degree. It won't ever be your strength, so make sure you stay out of situations that can cause problems for you. Know your limits.

I know one man on the autism spectrum who worked successfully for five years in a laboratory until he went drinking with his colleagues one night after work. In this informal setting, he could not handle the different level and type of social interaction with people who had no clue about his autism. He became drunk, acted inappropriately, and was promptly fired because he did not know his limits.

On the other hand, when you capitalize on your strengths and avoid situations for which you are not prepared, work goes more smoothly. I started my freelance design business after working for others for a while because I could manage my environment and social interactions more effectively this way. I can keep my work relationships on a technical level, so work is less stressful and more fulfilling for me.

The most successful work hard, are on time, constantly upgrade their skills, and try hard to get along with their colleagues.

Rule #2: Have a plan.

There are a few other things to remember about finding a job when you are on the autism spectrum. First of all, know what you want to do and get the necessary training and education for the job. For many of us on the spectrum, that entails developing talents we are born with. The best way to do that is to work closely with family members, teachers, counselors and others involved in your life. Then match your talents to the kinds of jobs that are available in your community. Work with your high school counselor to find out more about these jobs. Go to the Autism Society of America web page (www.autism-society.org), which has great information about transitioning from the school system into the workplace. Its most important message is that having a plan in place is critical.

The local community college or vocational technical school is another resource that should be used. These schools can open the door to many satisfying careers. Some really bright students may need to be taken out of the high school social pressure cooker and enroll at a university. This will enable them to find relationships through shared interests. College courses available over the Internet are another option. These classes are ideal for many people on the spectrum. Also, a high school student who is getting teased in school may be better off taking high school classes online and graduate that way. There are a lot of scams on the Internet, so when considering that option, always make sure that online courses are being taught by a reputable, accredited institution.

Don't stop planning when you get into the workforce. Keep up-to-date on the economy. Read your local newspaper, check the Department of Labor's *Occupational Outlook Handbook*, which is listed on the Department's web page (www.bls.gov/oco/) and is found in public libraries in the reference section. This will help you plan for your future.

Rule # 3: Develop a portfolio and show your work.

I am a firm believer in keeping a portfolio of copies of your best work, performance reviews, and other documents in your home rather than, or in addition to, your place of work. I talked to one person who lost a drafting design job.

Always make sure that online courses are being taught by a reputable, accredited institution.

Table 3.1: How to Make a Successful Portfolio

Many things can go into your portfolio, which should be gathered in an attractive notebook or folder. You can include:

- Color prints of graphic arts, work or web pages
- Copies of architectural and engineering drawings
- Copies of articles written in newspapers, magazines or newsletters
- Letters of reference
- Printouts of computer programs, spreadsheets or other work
- Photos of artwork or things you have built
- Scientific journal articles
- List of satisfied clients with references
- A resume with information on projects that you have completed
- Photos of products you have made, such as jewelry or woodworking
- Copies of papers you have translated – include both the original language and the translation

He had kept none of his engineering drawings to show to potential new employers. The only thing he had was an old unplayable disc for an obsolete computer system.

Print out paper copies of your best writing, drawings, PowerPoint presentations, computer programs, and other work. Keep copies of all performance reviews and letters that are complimentary. If possible, have electronic copies on hand so you can e-mail your portfolio.

When I first started my livestock design facilities business, I could get few others in that industry to take me seriously. What the engineers and designers saw was a woman (bad enough) with odd, off-putting mannerisms trying to talk with them about her ideas. They only would talk with me and take me seriously after I showed them my portfolio, a collection of drawings and designs.

"You drew these?" they asked skeptically. With a portfolio in hand, I could get their attention and eventually land some design jobs for my fledgling business. It was not easy and, at times, the process was downright rude and hateful. But I am here because I stuck it out and kept developing my design talent.

If you are in a field where showing your work isn't possible, you have to demonstrate what you are capable of doing in other ways. Sometimes you can show what you are capable of doing in volunteer jobs. Try working with someone you know in his or her business, just helping out in small ways at first. Volunteer at your church, synagogue, temple – all of the activities you take on when you are young can be used on your resume when you are older and job searching. Then your portfolio becomes your cover letter in which you explain and describe your concrete contributions to an organization.

Many people make the mistake of putting too much stuff in the portfolio. Pick out the best work. Five to 10 items are usually enough. Sometimes it is a good idea to have another person select your best work; this ensures more objectivity. Weird science fiction art is not the best thing to show an advertising agency that is hiring you to do car and bank ads. However, it would be the right thing to show if you were applying for a comic book artist job. Match portfolio content to the job, and even the employer. Only bring what will fit with the job for which you are applying.

Again, be prepared to have both a paper and electronic copy of your portfolio. In some cases, old-fashioned "snail mail" is most effective because people are afraid to open e-mail attachments that could infect their computer with viruses. Make sure your materials are presented neatly. Photos and drawings should be in a notebook in plastic sleeves. Get help from mentors, teachers, even the staff at the local printing shop may have some advice. Whatever you do, make sure it looks professional.

Rule #4: Develop your talents, no matter what they are, for they will help you in your job search.

Having strong talents is critical to your job search, so practice them consistently. At the same time, don't forget to practice your social skills, for those are terribly important as well. But the talent is the key. It is important to develop skills in things that other people want. Architectural drafting is a valued skill, for example, whereas playing video games is not a skill employers want unless you are super good at designing them. The video game design field is very competitive – there are probably 10 people for every video game design job.

> Having strong talents is critical to your job search, so practice them consistently.

Expect the unexpected. I got my first big client because of my sewing talent. I was wearing a western shirt I had embroidered when I met the wife of the insurance agent for a meat plant. She admired my shirt, and when I told her what I did for a living, she worked it out so I met with the plant president and presented my portfolio of designs. Of course, it was more than merely luck. By then I had been writing for *Arizona Farmer Ranchman* magazine and had been around the business for a while, so I knew the industry.

Rule #5: Be prepared to enter the job market through the back door, side door, any door but the front!

There are always more doors to enter than just the front door. This is a good rule to remember when looking for work and planning a career. Front doors to jobs are usually guarded by vigilant human resources departments, whose job is to screen applicants to fit a certain mold. People on the spectrum are often some of the first ones screened out of jobs because of their social eccentricities, lack of work experience, or gaps in their work history. You have to have a talent so strong and deep that it impresses anyone meeting you.

Since people on the autism spectrum tend to be good at one skill and not so good at others, I have concentrated this book on jobs that have a low barrier of entry. Algebra was impossible for me and foreign languages were difficult. My math disability locked me out of jobs in highly competitive fields such as veterinary medicine because I could not pass the entry exams. The veterinary medicine courses would have been fairly easy for me, but I could not get beyond the prerequisites.

While highly competitive fields such as medicine and veterinary medicine have a high barrier of entry, other jobs have a wide-open back door. For example, there are many people in the computer field who have no college degree. They were self-taught and they showed a portfolio of their work to the right person. The person who can open the back door for you may be found just about anywhere as illustrated above with the insurance agent's wife. These people may be at your church, bowling club, or living right on your block, so always be open and prepared to discuss these issues.

You have to be persistent to get in the back door.

You have to be persistent to get in the back door. I was rebuffed many times before I found the person who would open the back door. Be persistent, yet be polite. That is very important. In the food industry, for example, many eccentric and talented people got into satisfying jobs by starting out on boring jobs on the processing line. After learning many different skills, they started hanging around with the maintenance staff. When the maintenance staff saw their talent, they let them work with them. In another instance, a man who started digging ditches for fiber optic cable ended up a computer expert. During breaks, he hung around the computer people. The "back door" can work in many ways.

Consider freelance work if your talent lends itself to self-employment. Often people in design, computer programming or repair, construction, maintenance and similar fields can parlay their work into a business. Freelancing is not for the faint hearted, though, because you have to be able to market your product or service, manage your work flow, and keep good cash flow. Some individuals on the spectrum have been successful when they partnered with another person to run and manage the business. The talented person on the spectrum then works on assignments that are brought to him or her.

In some cases, I landed a design job by showing my portfolio to a guy I met on a plane. Maybe the person who can open the back door is in front of you in the supermarket checkout line. Politely introduce yourself to the fellow shopper who has a computer company badge hanging around his neck. In the early days of my career, I always had a few of my best drawings and photos of jobs in my purse. In brief, people are impressed with talent, and demonstrating your talent can often open up the back door.

Rule #6: Get to work on time, neatly dressed and with a good attitude.

This one sounds easy, but it can be difficult for people on the spectrum. Consistency at work is highly valued, and that includes getting to work on time and showing up with a cheerful, can-do attitude. Employers know they can teach the skills required for the job to their staff members, but they don't have the time to teach attitude. So, make it easy for

Consistency at work is highly valued, and that includes getting to work on time and showing up with a cheerful, can-do attitude.

Table 3.2: Using Computers to Teach Career Skills

Many adolescents are attracted to video games and spend an inordinate amount of time playing these games. The fast-moving animation is captivating for them and keeps them glued to the screen. The video games that are the most addictive are the shooting games with lots of rapid movement. These are the games that provide no useful skills for a career. I am not against all computer video programs. Unfortunately, most of the computer programs that enlighten and educate are expensive professional software. To use them, you would need to find a scientist, engineer, or other technical professional who would let you play with these "video games" that people use in their jobs. For example, scientists use fascinating programs for visualizing complex molecules in organic chemistry. Other programs convert flat drawings into three-dimensional virtual reality buildings that you can "walk through." Simulation software available in your local computer store can be used to motivate interest in how ecosystems work, for example.

---

them and come in with a good attitude and a willingness to try different things. After all, don't you want to work around people who are cheerful and pleasant?

The good thing about attitude is that it can be taught at a fairly young age by parents, teachers and counselors. My hat is off to those caring adults who take the time to help their youngster grow up independent and with a good attitude.

These rules for success have helped me over my years in the workforce, and I think they are just as true for others as they have been for me. Working is a wonderful experience, a human experience, and one to be treasured and be grateful for. It has been the bedrock in my life.

Conclusion

Just as in other parts of our lives, there are definite "rules" for success in the work world. For many people on the autism spectrum, these rules are particularly challenging due to their innate characteristics involving communication, emotions and social skills. Nevertheless, with proper preparation as outlined in this book, steps can be taken to ensure that one's true talents predominate – in other words, the focus here is on how to maximize your strengths. For those of us on the autism spectrum, there seem to be some general characteristics of successful individuals:

- ▶ Talent that was developed over time into skills that can be used in a career.

- ▶ Mentors who helped guide them through their confusing teen and young adult.

- ▶ Proper medication to help manage their sensory, anxiety or depression problems. (Note: There are some individuals who do not need medication.)

To be successful in the workplace as a person with autism spectrum disorders, please consider this advice as well:

- ▶ Know your strengths and limits

- ▶ Have a plan

- ▶ Create a portfolio of your work

- ▶ Develop your talents

- ▶ Be prepared to enter the job market through the "back" door

- ▶ Be on time and have a good attitude

Just as in other parts of our lives, there are definite "rules" for success in the work world.

CHAPTER 4

Finding a Vocation You Love

hoosing a career or vocation is one of the most important decisions people make in their lives. Because we spend so much time working, we want a job that is a good fit for our lives. We want something we can grow into, and that matches our strengths, interests, and lives. That is why it is so important to be careful about choosing your work.

In our increasingly complex world, jobs are also growing both more complicated and broad. So it's important to figure out what you do best, what you enjoy, before even beginning a job search. This takes time, but as you are about to find out in this chapter, there are some rather pleasant and "natural" ways to discover your vocational calling.

As we have emphasized throughout the previous chapters, cultivate your talent. You do this by paying attention to your interests, recording your observations, and talking with others about your shared interests.

Parents Play a Big Role

Parents play the most important role in the task of getting youths on the autism spectrum ready for the job world. If you are the parent of a child on the autism spectrum, help your child cultivate his or her strengths early on. How? By observing and listening and an awful lot of reflection. Notice his or her interests and passions – even if they seem a little off the wall or different. If your youngster is a whiz at taking

Choosing a career or vocation is one of the most important decisions people make in their lives.

Developing talents does not have to be expensive.

things apart, be sure to have plenty of Legos at home. Save boxes so your daughter can build a city, grocery store or a sculpture. For older children, science project kits are recommended. If you find your son plopped down on the ground studying an ant trail, get down with him and watch those ants at work. Learn about the natural world with him; check out books from the library, spend time outdoors walking that ant trail. Be delighted if your child is attracted to something like ants. With an interest in nature, children become explorers, opening up their lives even more. Children who spend most of their time playing video games do not learn skills that are useful for a career. I dislike video games because they are so addictive. I would never have developed my career if I had been addicted to video games, as discussed in Chapter 3.

Parents should carefully expand their children's horizon by starting with their interests and talents. It is these passions that will help them navigate the world. Don't do this alone, though. Incorporate other caring adults into this community, people who will take your child places, who can talk with her about their interests, and who can even help her discover new ones.

For myself, I loved to draw as a youngster and build things. When I was little, I built things from cardboard. Building skills learned as a child translated into building things from wood and steel as an adult. I loved using my hands to build and my visual thinking skills to design. Thankfully, my parents had the foresight to allow me to develop those talents by signing me up for classes, buying me books, and so on, and years later, I turned them into a paying vocation.

Developing talents does not have to be expensive. Community centers, parks and recreation departments, colleges, school districts, and other organizations provide low-cost, sometimes no-cost programs to the public. They also offer sports, arts and crafts, foreign languages, summer camps and other organized activities. For adults, colleges offer continuing education courses, ranging from computer skills to robotics to horsemanship. Many 4-H centers provide horsemanship training as well as other interesting programs for children and teens.

Cultivate Your Talents

I can't emphasize enough that people with high-functioning autism and Asperger Syndrome must be extremely talented in their vocation to make up for challenges in social skills. They have to be so good at what they do that people will want to buy their skills. They have to be so good at what they do that they are the last ones laid off during a recession because the employer does not want to lose their talents to someone else.

This is why parents have to start young with their children, supporting them in building their talents, teaching them about the world, and helping them navigate that world as best they can. That is why making a portfolio of your work – even as a youngster – is so important to the job search process. Start early. The more proof you have of your capabilities, the better off you will be in the workplace. And the more choices of places to work you will have.

Working with Your Child's School

Schools can be another resource for parents of children on the autism spectrum. If your son loves to draw, make sure the art teacher knows that. If music moves your daughter, tell that to the school music teacher. Early on, build relationships with the teachers whose expertise and interest match your child's. Do not leave out your child's classroom teacher. He or she can be a valuable resource for helping your child do well and thrive in school.

Schools sometimes focus on the deficits in students' lives, and not their abilities. That is a major mistake. Instead, schools must focus on helping students build on their strengths and work toward goals that will help them become successful. There are many talented individuals on the autism spectrum, but somehow along the way, often their talents were not cultivated and therefore did not flourish into paying jobs. That is a terrible waste.

Parents of children on the autism spectrum must keep an open, flexible mind about their children's abilities and motivations. Allow your children to spend time developing their fixations into hobbies. Encourage them in any way you can, for that will help.

> People with high-functioning autism and Asperger Syndrome must be extremely talented in their vocation to make up for challenges in social skills.

Mentoring

For many children and teenagers on the autism spectrum, schools are not always the friendliest places. Often, high-functioning teens misbehave in school because they get bored. So it's especially important to help your child find a mentor in his interest area to keep him learning and plugged into life.

I was lucky to have a wonderful high school science teacher, Mr. Carlock, who taught me how to do scientific research, a skill I have used repeatedly in my career and personal life. His mentoring helped steer me into a career that has combined my scientific and design interests. Mr. Carlock, like all good mentors, also encouraged me when the trials and tribulations of high school wore me down. Like others on the autism spectrum, I hyperfocused on pet subjects, which drove my fellow high school students and administrators nuts. The teasing was terrible, but Mr. Carlock's kindness and encouragement helped me get through and channeled those fixations into something larger than just myself – a vocation.

As I stated earlier, I was a poor student. The only subject I did well in was biology; I had no motivation to study English or history. Algebra was an incomprehensible mystery to me. My motivation in school improved when I realized that I had to study in order to be able to do the things I wanted to do. A good mentor can build motivation for schoolwork by using the motivation behind fixations. The one mistake that was made in my education was a futile attempt to learn algebra. I was never allowed to try trigonometry or geometry. I could have learned these with hands-on projects such as building a model bridge.

A mentor is one of the best kinds of help for those searching for a vocation. In a way, a mentor is a must for adults and teenagers on the autism spectrum because he or she can help them use their fixations in a positive way. Those fixations, researcher Leo Kanner (1971) notes, provide great motivation and can lead to careers and even a social life. Mentors help students discover and develop their talents, coach them in their decision-making and help them stay on task.

Schools and some workplaces offer mentorship programs, but mentors can be found just about anywhere. As mentioned, I found one of my first meat industry mentors

I channeled my fixations into something larger than just myself – a vocation.

when I met the wife of his insurance agent at a party. She liked my hand-embroidered western shirt, on which I had spent hours embroidering a steer head, and later helped me make the right connections.

Discover Your Strengths

There are other ways of discovering your strengths, and ultimately mentors as well. Author Richard Nelson Bolles suggests in *What Color Is Your Parachute?* (2003) that job seekers should study other people's lives and then ask themselves, "Now, whose job would I most like to have?"

Author Marsha Sinetar (1987) writes that adults seeking a career should leave enough time to discover their "right livelihood." Ideally, that should begin in childhood, but if it doesn't, there is still time. Start, Sinetar suggests, by noticing what you like, how you like spending your time, what activities give you energy – feed your soul in a way. Notice what individuals you pay attention to and what strikes you about them. Seek out role models and study their lives.

Study the lives of unique people to discover how they found their vocation, their work. Read biographies of people you admire. Many famous musicians and scientists were probably on the autism spectrum. How did they find their vocation? What steps did they take to make sure they were successful? Pay particular attention to how they found

> A mentor is one of the best kinds of help for those searching for vocation.

Table 4.1: Your Dream Job

To get started, try the following exercise.
1. Make a list of your first choices of jobs.
2. List your second and third choices as well.
3. List their job characteristics on separate pieces of paper.
4. Examine the lists and select the job that most interests you.
5. Find someone doing that job. Visit with him or her to find more out about the job; ask about likes and dislikes and take notes.
6. Get more ideas by studying everyone you know, have seen on TV or read about in newspapers. And take notes, so you can understand the information more thoroughly.

---

themselves. What values are important to them and how do they express them in their daily lives?

In the meantime, write about what you are noticing, both about the outside world and your own inner world. Keep a journal because by tracking your thoughts, you will discover your vocation in a timely – and interesting – fashion.

Notice what you like, how you like spending time, what activities give you energy.

Visit Interesting Workplaces

People with autism or Asperger Syndrome may get highly motivated if they visit a workplace that sparks their interest. If that is not possible, read the trade magazines from different industries or visit a trade show. Recently, I went to the Food Expo at McCormick Place Convention Center in Chicago and saw amazing machines that make ice cream novelties. As I walked through the show, I thought somebody had to invent these machines, and it is likely some of the inventors are on the spectrum. The Food Expo would be a great place to take a high schooler who was bored with school. There are things in the world that are more interesting than video games.

Conclusion

Finding a vocation you love is very important to your well-being. The process itself can also be very enjoyable. You'll learn a lot about yourself, about what's important to you and to your family. While in the midst of it, keep these points in mind:

▶ Cultivate your talent by practicing it as often as you can, whether it is art, chess, music, or writing. Parents, help your children find their talents early on in life.

▶ Be as talented as you can in your interest or chosen field, for that is the best way to find and keep a job you love.

▶ Study or observe people whose jobs interest you. Visit with them about their jobs and make sure to keep notes of your conversations and observations.

▶ Visit interesting workplaces, so you can learn more about the world of work.

In the next chapter, you'll find information about a job search process that is just as rewarding as the job you end up finding.

CHAPTER 5

Searching for an Ideal Job

I landed my first professional job while I was still in graduate school. It happened like this: At a rodeo I walked up to the publisher of the *Arizona Farmer Ranchman* magazine and asked if he would be interested in an article on squeeze chutes design. He was, so I wrote it up – "The Great Headgate Controversy" – and sent it off to him the very next week. The magazine published it, and I had my first job in the livestock industry.

I was still writing my thesis when all this happened, so freelancing was a great way for me to find out more about my chosen industry. I made a lot of contacts, learned more about the business of livestock facilities design, and figured out how to get my foot in the door. Publishing eventually led me to a job designing cattle chutes at a large feedlot construction company. Would I have gotten that job if I had not first worked as a freelance writer? Maybe, but it would have taken a lot longer, I bet. The contacts I made as a freelance writer allowed me to get to know the industry in a way I couldn't have as just a graduate student working on her thesis.

My point is that you have to get out and talk with people to discover the best jobs for yourself. In addition to researching and reading about careers, you have to spend some time visiting with people, asking them about their work in order to find out as much about careers and jobs as possible. That is what this chapter is about – the actual job search process. Even if you don't know your talents yet or what your career interests are, you can still follow this tried-and-true approach to finding the job for which you are best suited.

Get out and talk with people to discover the best jobs for yourself.

There are many ways to plan a career and find a job, but the process always starts with knowing your strengths and then identifying the job you want that fits those strengths. Chapter 4 discussed the ways to look for those career-building skills and abilities – your talents – and this chapter takes it one step further, to the job search process.

Start by reflecting on what you already know about your interests and strengths.

Know Yourself

The job search process can be confusing, but it can be pretty exciting. Not only are you seeking meaningful work, you are also getting to know more about yourself, what's important – and not important – for your life. That in itself is a great gift and great information to have.

Start by reflecting on what you already know about your interests and strengths. What brings you fulfillment? What piques your curiosity and energizes you so you want to jump out of bed each morning ready to start the day? I realize that these questions may sound odd in the context of the job search process. But once again, since we spend so much time working, we might as well make it enjoyable and fulfilling. Especially for those of us on the autism spectrum, having the right job can add such depth and beauty to our lives that is more than worth the effort it takes to figure out what will be the right livelihood for us.

To discover these more "hidden" elements of our lives, we sometimes need a spark to get us thinking. We can ask ourselves the questions, but we often need some outside help in understanding what's important. This outside help can take many forms, all the way from personality/traits questionnaires to sophisticated software programs found at college career centers, for example. These tools can provide a lot of good information, but ultimately they are just reflections of who you are. And after you take them, it is still up to you to use the information in such a way that it helps you determine your course of action.

If possible, visit different workplaces such as a research lab, architectural firm or construction company. There are probably many people at your church or school who could arrange a tour. Also, look at the trade magazines of different industries you think you may be interested in.

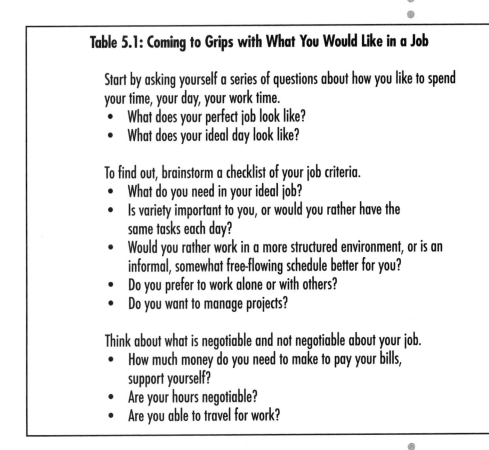

Table 5.1: Coming to Grips with What You Would Like in a Job

Start by asking yourself a series of questions about how you like to spend your time, your day, your work time.
- What does your perfect job look like?
- What does your ideal day look like?

To find out, brainstorm a checklist of your job criteria.
- What do you need in your ideal job?
- Is variety important to you, or would you rather have the same tasks each day?
- Would you rather work in a more structured environment, or is an informal, somewhat free-flowing schedule better for you?
- Do you prefer to work alone or with others?
- Do you want to manage projects?

Think about what is negotiable and not negotiable about your job.
- How much money do you need to make to pay your bills, support yourself?
- Are your hours negotiable?
- Are you able to travel for work?

Job criteria. To make the criteria in Table 5.1 as concrete as possible, write them out in complete sentences. Doing that will help you have a better understanding of what's important to you in a job. For example, you have decided you like to work with other people on projects, but you also need to work a fair amount of time by yourself. You could state that as: *I want to work in a team atmosphere, but definitely need to have my own office or work part of the time from home.*

If you know you are good at planning projects, you might say something like this: *I want to be in charge of creating and organizing projects that solve specific problems for clients and the organization.*

While writing down the criteria will help you focus on what's important to you in a job, writing down the statements in complete sentences helps you with the beginnings of a job description. Having that description makes the job search a hundred times easier and more fruitful. A surprising part of

By having
a written
checklist
and job
description,
you are less
likely to
become
stuck in the
sometimes
grinding
despair that
can go
along with
a job hunt.

this exercise is that once you have stated what you want in a job, synchronicity sets in. In synchronicity, your stated intentions attract people and opportunities to you that will help move along your job search. But that can't happen until you've made those intentions concrete by writing them down.

In other words, writing down what you want and need in a job makes it more likely you will be able to find that particular job.

Once you have brainstormed these qualities, organize them by their importance as follows:

▶ What must you have in your job?

▶ What would you like to have?

▶ What is negotiable?

Once you know what's most important in a job – the criteria you have established – you are ready to look at the job skills and abilities you possess that will help you land a job.

One added benefit of this kind of focusing effort is the psychological effect. It is calming, and that is usually desperately needed during a job search. By having a written checklist and job description, you are less likely to become stuck in the sometimes grinding despair that can go along with a job hunt. It feels good to have something concrete to work with. For instance, in any job I would do, I would have to be able to use my visual design skills. In addition, I would like to have a flexible schedule since I am also teaching at a college. Finally, travel is negotiable for me.

Features and benefits. Once you have figured out what you want and need in a job, you are ready to catalog the feature you have to offer.

Features refer to those skills, expertise, abilities and traits, credentials and work style you have to offer. The following exercise helps you identify the positive abilities you bring to a job. Also, by discovering these skills for yourself, you are in a better position to explain to employers or clients how you can benefit them.

Start by thinking of your core traits. Are you persistent, focused, attentive to details, and time conscious? Are you able to think through situations and come up with a plan to solve a problem? In the skills department, do you draw well, write well, work well with others? Are you creative, good with money, able to work alone and complete projects?

Now take those traits and skills – those specific abilities and expertise you have developed such as effective writing, instruction, or maintenance – and turn them into *benefits*, that is, the positive impact you can create for an employer, or clients if you are self-employed.

In a job interview or sales proposal, understanding how you can benefit someone's job, project or organization is very important. For instance, if you have determined one of your strengths is strong writing skills, you could say you would be able to save an organization time in preparing reports. Similarly, if you are particularly adept at problem solving, the benefit would be that you can smoothly move projects along and keep the work flow on an even keel. It is these kinds of benefits that will help you land the right job. It is the benefits that employers and clients are interested in – they are the concrete proof of your abilities and skills.

Table 5.2: Inventory of My Features and Benefits to Potential Employers/Clients

My Features
1.
2.
3.
4.
5.
6.

Benefits of My Features to Future Employer/Clients
1.
2.
3.
4.
5.
6.

Adapted by permission from J. Benjamin, B. Stanny, & K. Duffy. (1995). How to Be Happily Employed in Kansas City. Kansas City, Missouri: Career Management Press, p. 20.

Table 5.3: Sample Inventory of My Features and Benefits to Potential Employers/Clients

My Features
- 16 years' experience in teaching
- Strong writing skills
- Able to balance several projects at the same time
- Good at helping students and others understand new concepts
- Effective time management skills
- 8 years of mentoring experience

My Benefits
- Can develop and teach a wide variety of classes
- Am able to quickly analyze and address students' learning needs
- Can step into a new teacher's classroom, analyze the situation and collaborate on solutions
- Can produce effective reports and articles on a variety of subjects

---

In summary, my most unique feature and its benefit would be the ability to quickly analyze a classroom situation and help the teacher find a workable solution, saving the college the expense and hassle of having to hire a new instructor and ensuring students receive the education they deserve and need.

"30-second commercial." Never go to a job interview unless you have developed a list of benefits and are able to articulate them. To do so, try practicing a "30-second commercial" before you talk with potential employers. This exercise helps you focus on your strengths, and at the same time it gives you the confidence and self-assurance you need to get through what many people feel is one of the toughest situations they have to face. Arm yourself with this exercise and it will make your interview will go much better.

Prepare and then practice this exercise until you can get your crucial information down to 30 seconds. Shortness is key here, because employers, actually all of us, size up people we meet very quickly. So in a job interview, it is particularly important to get your message across as quickly as possible, and as polished as possible. You want to go into job interviews sounding poised and sure of your abilities – and,

---

Table 5.4: How to Create a "30-Second Commercial"

1. Determine what skills you want to use on the job: writing, drawing, planning.
2. Decide what job function you want to perform: sales, design, management, teaching, and programming.
3. List your strong interests or preferences: software design, program planning.
4. Define the kinds of problems you want to solve on the job: maintaining good communication flow with clients or employees; organizing new data for projects.
5. Describe the type of results you want to produce: creating improved databases for clients, designing effective web pages, maintaining heating and cooling equipment.
6. Describe the kind of environment you want to work in: use your job criteria list on (see pages 63-64). Do you like highly structured workplaces or do you work better in an informal environment with more autonomy?
7. Finish the following thought: "I know I can do this because I have _____ (cite specific work examples that highlight your features)."
8. List the direct results (benefits) of the above statement.
9. Practice your commercial and have someone videotape you, so you can perfect it.

Adapted by permission from J. Benjamin, B. Stanny, & K. Duffy. (1995). How to Be Happily Employed in Kansas City. Kansas City, Missouri: Career Management Press, p. 23.

---

most important, how those abilities will help the company you are approaching.

Get to Know Your Community

When planning a career, you have to know your "community," both the geographic and career communities. By getting to know the kind of jobs that are available in your area, profession, or field, you will have a much better chance of landing the kind of job you want. One of the best ways to do that is also one of the most enjoyable – informal interviewing.

Informal interviewing/brainstorming. In this kind of interviewing, you are simply finding out about different jobs in order to match your skills to a job description. You are ready for this step because you now know what's important in a job for you, and how your skills could benefit an employer or client. You may not know what job titles fit the kind of skills you possess, but you can find out simply by talking with others about their jobs

If talking with others is difficult for you, start practicing

Table 5.5: Example of "30-Second Commercial"

Outline

1. Three *skills* I want to use are planning, writing, and coaching.
2. The *job function* I want to perform is training.
3. My strong *interests* are course design and training.
4. The kinds of *problems I want to solve* are related to classroom instruction.
5. The type of *results* I want to produce are getting more teachers to use active learning and learner-focused curricula in their classes so students leave the college with an excellent education and a lifelong interest in learning.
6. The type of *environment* I want to work in is flexible and collaborative.

Final Version

I'm looking for a training position in a community college or other educational organization where my 16 years of planning, writing and training can make a difference in the quality of education students receive and the quality of teaching instructors provide.

I like working in a flexible environment where I have a lot of variety in my duties and can collaborate with my colleagues in developing student-focused curricula and programs that address how students learn most effectively.

In my past position as faculty mentor, I was responsible for training all new adjunct faculty through one-on-one mentoring sessions and regular professional development seminars that I developed, marketed and facilitated. For this job, I collaborated with faculty from all six divisions and conducted planning sessions with college Instructional and Student Services administrators.

now. Make a point of talking with a new person each day – not necessarily about your job search – but about other interests. Talk to people who actually do the work instead of the human resources department. Find out what being an artist, a librarian, or a programmer is really like. Many people you could interview would be people you see every day in your community. In the beginning, it is easier to start with people you already know. This kind of practice will prepare you for talking with others about your job search. Get as much practice as you need before you start talking about careers. But don't get so caught up in practicing that you can't get out the door to put it to work. Give yourself a deadline for getting started and have a trusted friend or family member "coach" you out the door.

By taking this very important step in career planning, you are not only finding out valuable information about careers in your community, you are also expanding your network of people who know you are looking for a career. In a sense, you are building a team of people interested in your job search, who are keeping their ears to the ground about job leads for you.

You are also creating your own personal database of job characteristics. By expanding your knowledge of the kind of jobs that are available in your community, you are making your own job search much easier. Start this step by making a list of everyone you know, friends, family, neighbors, and colleagues. This will speed up the job search process immensely, because most jobs are found through people we know, whether casually or closely.

Even if you have already worked in one field, keep an open mind to others. Just because you worked as a mechanic does not mean you have to continue working as a mechanic, but you should stay in a field that would use a mechanic's visual thinking skills if that's your special talent. For example, usually, accounting would not be an appropriate switch for a mechanic. By keeping your mind open to other careers

Table 5.6: List of Useful Contacts for My Job Search				
Name	**Address**	**Phone/E-Mail**	**Job Title**	**Relationship**

where your skills and abilities would be valued, you are expanding your job horizons. This is critical in our rapidly changing economy where people must keep up their skills in order to stay in the job market.

By conducting informal interviews, you will also get feedback on your presentation without it coming from a stranger, and you will get additional ideas about your goals, and often some pretty good advice on how to achieve them. To top it off, you will get names of people working in jobs that are interesting to you.

Even if you have already worked in one field, keep an open mind to others.

To prepare for an informal interview, it is often a good idea to have business cards and stationery letterhead printed. This is not necessary, or even appropriate, for every job, but if you are applying for a white-collar or professional job, that attention to detail will give the interview a more professional touch and also help you take on a job seeker's persona.

Write out a list of five questions to ask during the interview. You may end up asking more than five, but these will be your core questions.

When you contact your interviewees, ask if they would like you to send the questions to them ahead of time. Some people appreciate the extra time to think about an interview, so you are doing them a service – and, of course, you, too, are benefiting by preparing ahead of time. Try to get your interviews completed in about 30 minutes and let the interviewees know that is the timeframe you are aiming for. If it goes longer at the interviewee's request, that is fine – but it must be his or her decision.

For the interview itself, dress as you would for a regular job interview – neatly and conservatively. Find out from someone working in the same field how dressed up you have to be. For instance, if you are interested in auto repair,

---

Table 5.7: Questions to Ask During Informal Interviews

1. How would you describe your job?
2. How long have you been working in the field?
3. What kinds of changes in your field have you seen occur since you started, and what do you predict will happen over the next few years?
4. What's the best and worst attributes of your field?
5. What skills and abilities are important for your field?

do you have to wear a suit and tie to the informal interview? Probably not. Each profession has its own dress code, and you want to dress within the code – and always neatly.

Be on time and start the interview by thanking the person for spending the time with you, even if it is a close family member. This is good manners and is an important part of workplace culture. If this is your first job, it gets you in the practice of being in the workplace.

During the interview, make as much eye contact as you can and listen actively to the person with whom you are talking. Do not interrupt, but feel free to ask additional questions if the person talks about a topic that is interesting to you and concerns your job search. The latter is important. You must focus on the purpose of your appointment, not ramble all over the map; nor is this the time to perseverate on special topics or interests.

During the interview itself, take notes, whether through writing or taping. Many people don't feel comfortable being taped, so you must get their permission when you set up an interview time if you plan to tape them. If you are going to write notes, practice ahead of time. Only write the essentials; most of the time you want to be looking at the person, not at your notepad.

One of the most important pieces of information to come from an interview are the names of others to interview, as well as ideas and resources for your job search. Make sure you get the person's correct spelling and job title, if there is one; that is very important for a professional job search.

Finally, when it is time to go, thank the person again and shake his or her hand. Go over your notes as soon after the interview as you can. Highlight the most important information and add it to any kind of database you are keeping. Finally, be sure to send a short thank-you letter within a week of the interview.

Gathering background information. The other important way to learn about your community is by reading the local newspaper, business publications and any professional publications for the fields you are exploring. Make notes about businesses that look interesting, trends that would affect your job search.

For instance, you are really good at budgeting and tracking income and expenses, so you decide to go into book-

> One of the most important pieces of information to come from an interview are the names of others to interview, as well as ideas and resources for your job search.

keeping. However, you find out that one trend affecting small businesses – your target market – is the wealth of do-it-yourself financial software programs on the market. That trend means that small business owners could do their own bookkeeping, resulting in less business for you. By keeping up with these trends, or changes, you will be able to protect yourself better in our global marketplace by changing the focus of your services.

Although this sounds like a lot of work, the process of finding the livelihood that is right for you can be pretty enjoyable. You get to meet new people, expand your horizons, and learn about your community in the process. You will become an expert on careers in your particular area, community or town and may one day get to pass on that information to others.

Know Your Industry

The final step in locating a career or job for yourself involves learning about the field in which you want to work. In other words, after practicing informal interviewing to discover what kinds of jobs are out there, you are now narrowing your search, zooming in on specific jobs. This is where informational interviewing comes in.

Informational Interviewing. Through informational interviewing, you are able to find out about different employers and, sometimes, they are able to find out about you – without the stress of a real job interview. Once again, though, you are not to ask for a job during the interview; instead, you are to simply ask the interviewee about what he or she does on the job and about the trade or profession.

How do you get started? The following list will help get you going.

By treating this as a research project, your career search will be less stressful and more effective. Informational interviewing can be a low-stress, enjoyable venture that ultimately teaches you a lot about the job search process and about yourself as well.

Informational interviewing can be a low-stress, enjoyable venture that ultimately teaches you a lot about the job search process and about yourself as well.

Table 5.8: Steps in Setting up and Conducting Informational Interviews

1. Go back to the list of people and organizations you compiled in the informal interviewing stage and make a list of the people to whom you would most like to speak. Add to that list the names of people and organizations about which you have read in the newspaper as you did your community research. Write these individuals a letter, explaining your purpose and then make a followup telephone call to set up an appointment.

2. When you set up the time, make sure you tell the person you are not looking for a job with his or her organization but merely want to learn more. Then, make sure you never, never ask for a job during the interview.

3. Practice your interviewing technique with people you know before you head out for your first interview. Once you are ready for a "real" interview, go to people you know the best on your list or to people in a field that is less appealing to you. This will give you good, risk-free practice.

4. Prepare questions ahead of time and take them to the interview. Ask concrete questions, starting with the most basic one, "tell me what you do."

5. Although making small talk is not something individuals on the autism spectrum do well, it is necessary to start off the interview with relaxed conversation in order to build rapport with the interviewee. For example, ask how the person is, and then remind him or her why you are there and that you are not looking for a job from them at this time. Never go into sensitive topics. Relax as much as possible, for that will also make your interviewee relax. The interview will go better that way. Think of the interview as simply a "conversation" between interested individuals, for that is what it actually is.

6. Always, always leave at the agreed-upon time – unless your interviewee wants to extend the time. When you do leave, make sure you thank the individual in person, leave a business card, if appropriate. Also send a thank-you note within a week of the appointment.

7. Keep notes of your interviews, summarizing the information, including personal information that might be useful later on. Create a chart of information – potential employers, contacts, address/phone and referral source – by "area of interest" (see Table 5.9).

Table 5.9: Summary of Informational Interview

Name: _____

Position: _____

Company/Organization: _____

Referral Source: _____

Address: _____

Phone/e-mail: _____

Date	Type of Contact	Comments	Followup

Referrals, suggestions:

Resume sent: _____   Date: _____

Thank-you sent_____   Date: _____

Adapted by permission from J. Benjamin, B. Stanny, & K. Duffy. (1995). How to Be Happily Employed in Kansas City. Kansas City, Missouri: Career Management Press, p. 30.

Conclusion

Finding a job need not be the dreadful experience that many conjure it up to be. Think of it as a way to not only become employed, but to learn about your community and become a meaningful part of it. To find a job that "suits" you, try these steps:

▶ Know yourself – Take some time to discover what you do best in life, reflect on how to turn your talents into paying jobs. Write about your discoveries and observations in a journal or record your thoughts about them into a tape recorder.

▶ Know your community – Who do you know that could help you navigate the job market? Make a list of family friends, church, temple, synagogue members, neighbors, teachers – all the people you know – and start talking with them about their jobs. What do they like and what don't they like about their work? Keep good notes.

▶ Know your industry – Read about your field, interview people working in the field to find out about the ups and downs of the job. When you have gathered all this information, make sure you write your "30-second commercial" to use in job interviews.

It's important to know what jobs are good matches for you and what's out there in your community and industry. The next step is to take that information and explore the field. In Chapter 6, we will cover an important area in your job search, the types of jobs that are best suited for the thinking styles of individuals on the autism spectrum. You'll also be reading about the global economy that affects all of our jobs these days and some ways to keep up with it.

It's important to know what jobs are good matches for you and what's out there in your community and industry.

CHAPTER 6

Do What You Do Best

Before you actually land your first job as an adult, there are two very important pieces of information you must have. One has to do with how you "think," the other concerns the economy in which you live. If you can work at a job that matches how your brain processes information, you will be better off in the long run. At the same time, the more you know about the economy, the easier it will be to navigate it. This chapter has information on both those topics.

The Way You Think

Know how you process information. I personally think in pictures, not words. That is, when I hear spoken words, I immediately, without knowing it, translate them into pictures in my mind. While that may sound odd, I have found that there are many of us – on and off the autism spectrum – who think this way. We are "visual thinkers."

For instance, when one of my clients tells me about his concerns about a livestock chute design, I immediately turn those words into a movie in my head, view it and then store it in my "mental file cabinet." Here the information goes into my long-term memory available for me to pull back up when I need it again.

Thankfully, I have excellent long-term memory, the storage unit in the brain. At the same time, I have very bad short-term working memory. For example, if I try to do two or three things at the same time, I will get frazzled. Therefore, for me to

If you can work at a job that matches how your brain processes information, you will be better off in the long run.

be in a job that requires that kind of "multitasking" would be pure disaster. I am not alone. Most people on the spectrum, whether high- or low-functioning, have poor short-term working memory, but often they have better long-term memory than most people.

Autism/Asperger brains tend to be specialized. I have noticed they tend to be good at one thing and not so good at something else. In general, there are three different specialized brains: (a) visual thinking, thinking in pictures; (b) music and higher-math brains; and (c) verbal lists and language translator brains (Grandin, 1999). Following are lists of jobs that use the talent of each type. These are jobs that would be careers instead of just jobs. These are also jobs that have a low barrier of entry when compared to medicine and law, for example.

The first group, jobs for visual thinkers, requires little abstract math and hardly any multitasking that relies on the fast information processing that occurs in short-term memory. Instead, they utilize visual thinking and long-term memory, two major strengths for individuals on the spectrum. These jobs would also be good for people with dyslexia. Many dyslexics are visual thinkers, and they also have problems with multitasking.

Table 6.1: Jobs That Would Be a Good Fit for Visual Thinkers

- Architectural and engineering drafter
- Photographer
- Animal trainer
- Graphic artist
- Jewelry maker and other crafts
- Web designer
- Veterinary technician

- Auto mechanic
- Machine maintenance technician
- Computer troubleshooter
- Theater lighting director
- Industrial automation programmer
- Landscape designer
- Biology teacher

Music and math minds think in patterns of numbers or musical patterns. Children with this kind of thinking often have a knack for music, and math is easy for them. They tend to be nonvisual thinkers who are good with numbers, facts and music. See Table 6.2 for sample jobs.

Table 6.2: Jobs That Would Be a Good Fit for Music/Math Brains

- Computer programmer
- Engineer
- Physicist
- Musician/composer
- Statistician

- Math teacher
- Chemist
- Electronics technician
- Music teacher
- Scientific researcher

Table 6.3 lists jobs that generally are well suited for nonvisual thinkers who are good with numbers, facts and foreign languages; in other words, people with more verbal brains. When they were young, they were interested in lists and numbers. An example of a common childhood interest would be memorizing all the baseball batting averages. These jobs also put little demand on short-term working memory, but do require excellent long-term memory.

Table 6.3: Jobs That Would Be a Good Fit for Nonvisual Thinkers with More Verbal Brains

- Journalist
- Translator
- Librarian
- Stocks and bonds analyst
- Copy editor
- Accountant

- Budget analyst
- Bookkeeper and record keeper
- Special education teacher
- Book indexer
- Speech therapist
- Inventory control specialist

The types of jobs that are very bad for both high- and low-functioning people on the spectrum are those that require multitasking, doing several things at one time. I would have difficulty doing many entry-level jobs such as being a cashier that require making changes while talking to a customer. Taking dictation would be difficult due to auditory processing problems. Also, working as a receptionist would probably be a very bad job for me because so many things would be going on at once. In general, we need jobs that involve doing one task at a time.

Follow Your Interests

When you are thinking about the kind of work you want to do, follow your interests but be practical, too. If you go to college, pick a major that is likely to lead to a job. For example, computer science is generally a good choice. In fact, I am convinced that many of the best programmers have Asperger Syndrome or at least some of its traits such as poor social skills and obsessions with a single topic.

Other good majors for individuals on the spectrum include accounting, engineering, library science, and art with an emphasis on commercial art and drafting (to ensure making a living). Generally, majors in history, political science, business, English or pure math should be avoided. It is very difficult to find jobs with just those degrees. However, you could major in library science with a minor in history, as the library science degree would make it easier to get a good job.

If you are the parents of young people on the autism spectrum, please encourage your teenager to take college-level courses in drafting, computer programming, commercial art or other subjects of interest while still in high school. This can help these students stay motivated at a time when life can feel pretty confusing.

Social Skills

You also need to learn or polish some social survival skills – listening, eye contact and conversational skills to start with. The workplace is a social institution, and politeness and grooming count for a lot. There also can be stiff competition for jobs, and the more polished you are, the better you will do. I realize this is not easy for those of us on the autism spectrum, but it's important to at least try. More than likely, you will make friends at work by talking about your shared interests. My social life is almost all work-related. That is, I am friends with people I do interesting work with.

As mentioned earlier, to survive in the workplace, you must learn diplomacy. Even if the boss is acting badly, do not tell him or her so. For that matter, bluntly telling colleagues they are acting badly will not help your cause either. It is important to learn how to tell people negative things without insulting them. Separating the offending behavior from the

> When you are thinking about the kind of work you want to do, follow your interests but be practical, too.

person is a good first step. Protecting yourself from the problems of coworkers is a second step.

Financial and Other Record Keeping

Other survival skills you must have include learning how to handle your finances and proper record keeping. For instance, when I get a bill, I pay it the day I get it, so I don't forget. For my business, I also had financial experts show me how to create the necessary records to track my income and expenses. I charge flat rates for my services and mark the payments and the job itself on my checkbook stub. That keeps the record keeping easy, and then I am more successful at it.

The 21st-Century Economy

The second piece of information you need before looking seriously for a job or career is what is going on in the economy in general. You need to know this so you can be prepared for the ups and downs of our global economy. One of the hallmarks of the economy in the 21st century is innovation. Innovations are constantly bringing changes in how we run our business, schools and our lives.

Knowledge Economy

Basically, the 21st-century economy can be summed in one word: Technology. Technology has drastically changed the workplace, from manufacturing plants to school rooms to small offices. It has sparked new life into the American economy and created new types of jobs. But it has also taken away some of the manual, nontechnical jobs that people on the autism spectrum and others would have performed. This makes understanding the economy more important today than even 10 years ago.

You will be living and working in this global economy for the rest of your life, so you must educate yourself about it, beginning in your school days. Read as much as you can in your daily newspapers and national publications such as *Business Week, Newsweek, Time, Fortune, Forbes* and *The Wall Street Journal.*

We live in what's called a "knowledge economy." Information and education are now valued most. Not surpris-

> One of the hallmarks of the economy in the 21st century is innovation. Innovations are constantly bringing changes in how we run our business, schools and our lives.

The 10 fastest growing occupations require some form of post-secondary education to even step into them.

ingly, if you look at the United States Department of Labor's *Occupational Outlook Handbook,* you will find that the fastest growing jobs are all technology-related. Information and communication drive our world now.

The growth industries in the United States are in the "Services" category. Three out of five new jobs come from this category, which includes finance, insurance, real estate, government, transportation, communications and utilities. Most of those new jobs will be in business, health, and social services. You will find the fast growing technology jobs listed in the "Business Services" category.

Lifelong Learning

The 10 fastest growing occupations require some form of postsecondary education to even step into them: medical assistants, network systems and data communications analysts, physician assistants, social and human service assistants, home health aides, medical records and health information technicians, physical therapist aides, computer software application engineers, computer software systems engineers, and physical therapist assistants (www.bls.gov/news.release). "Education is essential in getting a high-paying job," reads the latest edition of the *Occupational Outlook Handbook.* "In fact, all but two of the 50 highest paying occupations require a college degree." What this means for your future is that you must get some kind of postsecondary training, whether it is through a community college, vocational school, university or job training center in order to get a job in today's economy. You need to know how to learn and know that you will be learning all your life.

Where we once went to school only in our youth, we now have to be lifelong learners in order to keep up with the changes that are constantly occurring around us. For some, that means getting on-the-job training; others may attend classes or log on to online classes. Whatever the mode, education is a lifelong matter now. You will not only be learning on the job, but in schools and seminars as well. It is simply a fact of life that lifelong learning is with us to stay.

When planning for a career or job, do what you do best. You want to build from your strengths and work in fields that capitalize on those strengths. If you have strong talents, be sure to make a portfolio of your work. A portfolio, whether in paper or electronic form, is a good tool for your job search. In addition, learn as much as you can about today's global economy to better prepare yourself for working in it. Finally, remember to always, always sell your work, not your personality.

In the final chapter of this book, you will meet individuals from a wide range of jobs and careers especially selected as potentially suitable for individuals on the autism spectrum.

We now have to be lifelong learners in order to keep up with the changes that are constantly occurring around us.

CHAPTER 7

Best Jobs for Individuals on the Autism Spectrum

*T*his chapter presents the stories of individuals working in fields that would be good for many on the spectrum. They have some excellent advice about how to get into those fields and stay there. In addition to first-hand experience, the profiles include career information from the U.S. Department of Labor's *Occupational Outlook Handbook*.

The interviewees were selected because of their experience in the professions or fields chosen as good fits for many on the autism spectrum. They were interviewed in different ways: by telephone, in person and by e-mail. Sometimes all three methods were used for one profile.

The interviewee below, Sara Miller, is an entrepreneur who is on the autism spectrum herself. Her career story is a good example of the many different paths and routes people follow in discovering a career that fits them.

The Career Journey of One Person on the Spectrum

Sara Miller – Industrial/Manufacturing Computer Programming

Sara Miller was diagnosed with pervasive developmental disorder not otherwise specified (PDD-NOS) in 1992, before the term "Asperger Syndrome" was used in the United States. She operates her industrial/manufacturing computer programming business in Minneapolis. This is her story of her career journey.

How did you get into your career?

My difficulty with this question is the definition of what is my "career."

The development of my career was done more by others – they saw skills and recommended ways of using them. I tried the suggestions and usually succeeded, probably because of my phenomenal literal memory. For as long as I can remember, I have been "mimicking others," or doing what is expected of me by others. Until recently, I never really thought about what it was that I – me – Sara – really wanted to do. That said, here's the progression.

In my junior year of high school (East High School, Green Bay, Wisconsin, 1970-71), the most respected science teacher recommended that I participate in a National Science Foundation summer school program. I attended the program in biochemistry, an intensive six-week residential program in Windsor, Connecticut. I remember it was great being around 49 other smart kids from across the country. We had a group research project, which I continued when I returned for my senior year. I won the Green Bay science fair that year, possibly because some of the judges couldn't even pronounce the title of my project, "Degradation of a Heteropolysaccharide." My sponsoring teacher was proud, but also disappointed that I didn't enter in state, regional or national contests. I didn't see the connection between goofy science fairs –where you had to talk to new and strange people – and scholarships, schools and future careers. Nevertheless, the experience left me with the feeling, "Well, I could always do something in the science field ..."

I started college at the University of Minnesota because my parents had gone there. Things did not work out, however, probably because I was having trouble meeting new people. Midyear I decided to transfer to University of Wisconsin-Madison, where many of my friends were going. In the meantime, at the suggestion of a girl down the hall in the dorm, I took a class called Nutrition for Non-Majors. I had a blast in that class because I knew most of the content already. My mother was trained as a physical therapist and brought us up with a strong health consciousness. I said to myself, "I can get a major in this?? What a piece of cake!!" So, upon transferring, I declared Nutrition & Food Science as my major.

After graduation (Dec. 1975) I went to work in the food industry. Everyone thought it was a great field to enter, since everybody has to eat, even in bad economic times. My ability to handle a significant amount of data and my obsession for exactness led me into the quality control (QC) area of the production facilities. Not a bad place for an OCD/autistic!! However, I became very upset when others wouldn't "follow the rules," and would end up quitting and finding another food industry/QC job, until I became disenchanted with the next group of people.

In the late 70s and early 80s, computers were being installed into food manufacturing machines. Again, because of my logic/binary skills combined with a great memory, I was assigned to help develop the specifications for automating various processes. Then I was assigned to learn how to program the special industrial computers. Another piece of cake for me!!

After running circles around my boss and his peers, I again was disenchanted with the intellectual level. With my lack of social skills and sometimes strange responses or behavior, I didn't know how embarrassing I was to these people. In my mind, all I was doing was stating facts. Corporate loved me and wanted to promote me. The locals wanted me fired. So I quit ... again.

Since I had been introduced to the industrial programming field and most people thought I was an engineer anyway, I decided to return to school to work on a Computer Engineering Technology associate degree from Milwaukee School of Engineering (MSOE). The first years of engineering classes follow a certain technical sequence. Since I already had a degree, I didn't need to take any of the general studies courses. So, I filled up my time teaching Quality Control & Statistics courses for MSOE in the Continuing Education Department. I also started to freelance my already developing programming skills as an independent contractor.

After the course of study was completed, I did not pursue a formal job with an established company. The independent contractor situation suited me just fine – I could focus on the details of solving customers' problems and, when done, I could get the heck out of there, thus avoiding any involvement with political games and silly chitchat with coworkers.

It was during this phase that I was diagnosed with PDD–NOS. I also met Temple that first year, and we were amazed at how similar the structures of our businesses were. We both worked as single persons operating a business out of our homes.

Except I wasn't smart enough to leave well enough alone ... My father was a successful entrepreneur and my mother saw to it that her five daughters were trained in the manners and etiquette of being presentable in public. Those skills, along with that good memory again, led others to suggest that I should start another company designed for a small group of industrial contractors or consultants who shared administrative assistance. In January 1995, NOVA Systems Inc., an industrial systems integration firm, was started.

The ups and downs of small company ownership now entered my life. It was much more emotionally difficult than I had anticipated, and I was not prepared. The typical people skills of independent contractors don't lend themselves to teamwork. So, in summary, I'm happy if my "career" is considered to be an industrial/manufacturing programmer. I'm not so happy with – and definitely would not recommend for people with ASD – ownership of a business that has several employees.

Describe your field or industry and the trends affecting it

Industrial automation or systems integration is my field. Over the last two decades, as the price for hardware has come down, there are more opportunities for acceptable return on investment for retrofitting older machines with the newer electrical controls. However, in down economic times, machines are allowed to limp along with their old methods, and business can be slow. We are now entering an upswing, which will help the industry as a whole.

Another fact affecting the industry is overseas competition. With the continued development of the capabilities over the Internet, U.S. integrators/programmers have to be really good and sell on their proximity for quick service. The good news is that many high-level members of the autistic spectrum are very good at this type of activity.

What is your advice to someone wanting to break into your field or industry?

As a programmer: Learn something else besides programming. Programming is just logic. Programming is only "translating" human stuff into a set of binary bits (a language) that a machine understands. If you learn French, but never go to France, how do you expect to know the nuances of culture in your communication? Likewise, in computer programming, your ability to program successfully depends on your understanding of the foundational body of knowledge of the "human" subject. For example, I intimately knew the food-manufacturing systems before I found out that "programming" existed.

As an engineer: To work in industrial automation, you have to be well rounded in mechanical, electrical, and industrial engineering – or at least have really good "friends" on whom you can rely for technical advice.

How do people get promoted in your field or industry?

Truly, a piece of paper confirming a B.S. in engineering is not needed to be successful, but you'll have a hard time getting past the human resources department at many companies without it. Also, various forms of that piece of paper will help with advancement and salary increases if you want to be in management. Much of the technical details can be taught on the job if you have an understanding of physics, motion and electricity. Industrial products are generally technologically ahead of what is presented in most schools.

The skills and talent that are needed include:

▶ Logic: ability to organize lots of data

▶ Detail oriented: ability to see the effects of the small stuff

▶ Creative: ability to look at things from a different viewpoint

▶ Quizzical: asking lots of questions to understand the total picture

▶ Unending desire to learn more: ability to self-teach

Resources

There are gazillions of trade magazines. Here are a few I like:
> *Control Engineering*
> *Industrial Computing*
> *Manufacturing Automation*

Web Sites

> www.automationtechies.com
> www.control.com
> www.manufacturing.net/ctl/

Professional Organizations

> American Society for Quality, www.asq.org
> Instrument Society of America, www.isa.org
> Society of Manufacturing Engineers, www.sme.org
> Institute of Electrical and Electronics Engineers (IEEE), www.ieee.org

Meet People on the Job and Learn From Their Experiences

In the best of all possible worlds, a kindly family member would take you by the hand and teach you about the many different kinds of jobs that are out there. In fact, a family member may have done that very thing with you. However, the world of work is a broad and complex place, so it is beneficial to have as many helping hands as possible.

Think of this next section as just that – a series of helping hands that belong to some very talented people who are taking the time to share what they know about careers in their field or industry. Use their experience and know-how to learn more about these professions that range from aircraft engineer to veterinarian assistant.

While you're reading, pay close attention to the following:

▶ In the **Introduction**, notice the background information about the career. This came from the very helpful U.S. Department of Labor's *Occupational Outlook Handbook*. Salary range and growth rate are listed, but the handbook has far more information, both on its web page (www.bls.gov/oco/) and in the book form found in just about every public library in the country. You can get a lot more information from that source.

▶ Next, read the **Insider Advice** section that details the interviewee's perspective on the changes occurring in the field or career and the skills and abilities you will need to do well in that occupation.

▶ Then you will want to study the **Breaking In** section, which details the kind of education or experience you need to even step into a job in that field.

▶ In **Success on the Job**, you'll find advice on how to get promoted in that field, what employers look for in their staff members.

▶ The **Resources** section details the trade publications and associations for that field as well as similar professions.

At the end of the book, in the Appendix, is list of additional career resources, books and organizations that will make your job search more fruitful. Happy reading!

PROFESSION **AIRCRAFT MECHANIC**

Azlan Hazeman

INTRODUCTION As a young boy, Azlan Hazeman loved to ask a lot of "why and how" questions. Why was the sky blue? How did the fan's blades keep from falling off? Why does electricity power the appliances? That curiosity – and persistence, his mother would probably add – led him into a perfect occupation for such an inquisitive mind: aircraft maintenance engineer.

For the past 10 years, Hazeman has been relying on this native inquisitiveness and mechanical ability to find and fix problems with the huge aircraft parked in his airline employer's hangar.

"It is my responsibility to ensure that aircraft are serviceable and airworthy before they are being released to service," Hazeman says. "To be more specific, when an aircraft enters a hangar check after flying a certain number of flying hours, my job is to rectify any defects reported by the pilots and carry out scheduled maintenance inspection checks and operational tests as stipulated by the manufacturer's maintenance schedule."

This can include the repair, replacement, overhaul, inspection and testing of the aircraft's electrical and instrumentation, engine and aircraft system. As an aircraft maintenance engineer, Hazeman supervises a team of mechanics, whose work he must certify before the aircraft can be flight ready.

The median hourly salary for mechanics and technicians was $19.50 in 2000. The 2003 *Occupational Outlook Handbook* reports that the aircraft mechanic field should be healthy over the next 10 years, with most job opportunities occurring at small commuter and regional airlines, Federal Aviation Administration repair stations, and in general aviation. Students just beginning their training are in luck, for there will be less competition for jobs during this time period. With fewer military personnel entering the field and a large number of retirements, there is simply less competition for jobs.

INSIDER ADVICE The most sought-after jobs are with large airlines, which offer higher pay and travel benefits. You need some pretty strong work experience, though, to be eligible for those positions, and a track record of keeping up with the technological changes in the field. Further, the competition for those jobs should heat up as airlines continue to consolidate and adopt automated inventory control systems.

According to Hazeman, "In general, there are not many trends that directly affect this field apart from our aircraft maintenance practices and the performance of our parent company. If the business is running well, we'll be very busy with maintenance. If the world economy is not good, as happened during the SARS epidemic, for example, some of our aircraft will be grounded, leaving us in standby mode."

To do well in this field, first, understand the theory behind the aircraft system very well and, second, have adequate experience fixing various defects and troubleshooting problems. The more you have worked on normal and abnormal aircraft defects, the faster you will be able to fix them. If you come to the airline with a lot of experience and a deep understanding of aircraft systems, you'll spend less time checking the manual. You'll save the airline a lot of time and money because aircraft will be able to depart on time.

"A successful engineer is one who can carry out necessary tasks and rectify defects on time," Hazeman says, "plus manage the mechanics working under him or her."

In high school, get a strong background in mathematics, physics and English in order to understand aircraft theory. The rest will be taught during the four years of training, which includes on-the-job and in-class training. Physical fitness and health are also necessary to be able to work the three rotating (day, evening and night) shifts and to be able to handle the physical rigors that go along with the job. You do a lot of climbing and walking as an aircraft mechanic or engineer.

BREAKING IN

To be promoted in this field depends on seniority and experience with many types of aircraft. Normally, promotions include becoming lead engineer, foreman, or superintendent. In general, these positions are over the entire aircraft maintenance crew (engineers, mechanics and apprentices) to ensure that teamwork and cross-functional responsibilities are being handled satisfactorily.

SUCCESS ON THE JOB

RESOURCES

It is compulsory, of course, to read inspection notices or aircraft manufacturers' bulletins of current issues, so that you can keep up-to-date on any problems with existing aircraft and the development of new aircraft.

For more information about this field, contact:

▶ Professional Aviation Maintenance Association
1707 H St. NW, Suite 700
Washington, DC 20006

If aircraft mechanic jobs appeal to you, you may also be interested in other mechanical jobs such as:

▶ Auto mechanic
▶ Heating and air conditioning installation
▶ Electrician
▶ Copier repair
▶ Industrial equipment maintenance

ARTIST

Bernadette Torres

With only 147,000 people in the United States working as artists, you would think this would not be a competitive field. But, in reality, it is just the opposite. To work as an artist you not only have to be talented, you also have to be very passionate about what you do to make a go of it.

Or as ceramist Bernadette Torres says: "You have to do your art every day!"

More than half of the artists in the United States are self-employed, about seven times the proportion in similar occupations, according to the *Occupational Outlook Handbook*. Ask any self-employed person what it takes to be successful, and you'll hear over and over: passion, drive and organization!

Besides being self-employed, artists also work for organizations as teachers, art directors, animators, multimedia artists, illustrators, painting restorers and a host of other jobs. With technology such a huge part of our world, artists are also putting their talents to work creating special effects, animation and other visual images for video, film, computers and other electronic media. In other words, artists do it all!

Employment for artists is expected to grow as fast as the average for all occupations between 2000 and 2010, about 10-20 percent, the *Occupational Outlook Handbook* reports. Annual salaries for fine artists who worked for organizations and businesses, including painters, sculptors and illustrators, vary widely, ranging all the way from a low of about $14,000 to more than $58,000. Art directors earned between $30,000 and $110,000; multimedia artists' earnings ranged between $23,000 and $70,000. All of the above figures were reported in the *Occupational Outlook Handbook*.

Bernadette Torres has been making art since she was a small girl in St. Petersburg, Florida. Her "working career" began in the fourth grade. When her family could not afford the tuition for her art program at an after-school youth center, the teacher "hired" her as a teacher's assistant.

"I even won Volunteer of the Month for my work," Torres laughs. "The mayor gave me a plaque."

Torres is a ceramist who also is on the art faculty at a college. She went into teaching after holding a number of different kinds of jobs. "I missed working with students a lot," she says.

She attributes her drive to be an artist to a number of excellent teachers who encouraged her throughout her school years. With her instructors' help, Torres learned to always do her best work and to be professional. That is something she advises all budding artists to do as well.

BREAKING IN Training and education vary by art specialty, but, in general, some formal postsecondary education is necessary to work as a fine artist. Many colleges offer bachelor in fine arts programs as well as master's degrees. These programs focus more on studio work, but having a solid grounding in core subjects such as English, math, social science and the natural sciences is also important.

Torres found that although her college prepared her well for her work as an artist, it did not do so well in training her for a "career" in art. When she wanted to go to graduate school, she found she had a difficult time writing the necessary letters and essays.

"I may have had a difficult time with writing, but I knew who to turn to for help," she says. "I wrote what I needed to say, and then went to friends who were in journalism and other fields to help me refine it."

Art schools are doing a better job now of teaching general education subjects to their students, Torres says. To teach fine arts on the college level, you must have a master's degree. For elementary and secondary schools, a teaching certificate and bachelor's degree are necessary. Other art jobs such as illustrators and art directors have their own educational routes, so be sure to check the Department of Labor's the *Occupational Outlook Handbook* for that information.

For many art jobs, you will need to build a portfolio. Always, always document your artwork with photographs, Torres advises. She also suggests young artists try everything, learn how to do a variety of different art forms and jobs. Once desperately needing a new job, Torres took the advice of a friend who said, "Become a costume designer; all you do is glue on sequins."

So she went to the *Yellow Pages*, found seven costume design firms and sent off photographs of costumes she had designed for herself over the years to the firms. Within days, she had an interview and was hired as a costume designer – even though she didn't know how to sew, a big part of the job. "I learned to sew on the job," Torres says.

First of all, Torres advises, be professional. And always, always ask for what you want. Learn how to talk with people, even if you are shy. That talking will help you find opportunities within your field as well as build connections with people who are interested in your work.

Keep doing your art every day, even if you have a day job that doesn't involve art. Be visible with your work and apply for grants, fellowships, scholarships, competitions, everything. It will help promote your work as well as provide additional revenue.

Finally, Torres advises, know your business, whether that is the freelance art business, design industry, or animation field. Know it inside and out, for it will help you do well and love your work even more.

For information about art and design, check out:

▶ The National Association of Schools
of Art and Design
11250 Roger Bacon Dr., Ste. 21
Reston, VA 20190
www.nasad.arts-accredit.org/index.jsp

If being an artist appeals to you, you might like art talent jobs such as:

▶ Architectural or engineering, drafting and design
▶ Graphic design
▶ Jewelry making
▶ Web page design
▶ Commercial art for advertisement

PROFESSION   **COLLEGE PROFESSOR**

Stephen Shore

INTRODUCTION   If you are interested in teaching at a college or university, you are in luck. Those institutions along with other postsecondary educational institutes are busy places these days for a number of reasons, including the federal government's welfare-to-work mandate; an increase in the number of 18- to 24-year-olds in the population; more adults attending college for job training; and an increasing number of international students attending American institutions. There's more good news: teaching jobs at these postsecondary institutions are expected to grow faster than the average for all occupations through 2010, according to the *2002-2003 Occupational Outlook Handbook*.

Postsecondary education includes a variety of teaching positions, ranging from those that require a Ph.D., such as at a four-year college or institution, to vocational-technical positions in institutes and schools that specialize in training students for specific careers. In 2000, there were more than 1.3 million postsecondary educators, the bulk of them working as faculty members teaching the nearly 15 million full- and part-time students in America's four-year universities and colleges and in two-year community college systems.

The median annual earnings for postsecondary instructors were $46,330.

INSIDER ADVICE   Like many other professors, Stephen Shore's career encompasses much more than his teaching duties at a college in Boston, where he is on the music faculty. Shore, who is on the autism spectrum, does consulting and writing in addition to making presentations about autism and Asperger Syndrome. Echoing the trends mentioned above, the biggest changes Shore has seen in his teaching career is that the student body is becoming increasingly diverse in terms of age, culture, and nationality. In addition, Shore points out, more and more students with disabilities of all types are enrolling in postsecondary institutions. As a result, educators must learn more than ever before how to teach to the students' strengths.

"We are in the business of education, so we have to broaden our repertoire of teaching methodologies and assessment,"

Shore says. "We have to get away from 'downloading' data into students' heads and having them regurgitate."

Good teachers must be more like facilitators, Shore says. Other necessary strengths and skills include being able to:

▶ Organize and present information in a variety of ways in order to teach to students' various learning strengths.

▶ Make a connection with students, determining their skill and ability levels, and creating a class curriculum with those in mind.

▶ Teach on multiple skill levels, for classrooms are full of students with varying strengths, backgrounds, and abilities.

▶ Use a variety of technology in the classroom, including computers, CD-ROMs, and software programs as teaching aids.

▶ Keep abreast of one's field and incorporate new research and information into teaching.

▶ Serve on academic and administrative committees.

▶ Advise and counsel students about their degree programs and career choices.

▶ Supervise graduate students' teaching and research and conduct one's own research projects, if in a four-year institution.

BREAKING IN

To teach for a community college's general education programs, you need at least a master's degree in your field. Vocational teachers often just have an undergraduate degree and experience in their field, whereas university faculty members must have a doctoral degree. Generally, four-year universities and colleges stress research more than the "art of teaching," so if you are interested in working with students, the two-year community colleges may be your best bet. Many instructors learn the business of teaching by working at it part time, which is also an excellent way of knowing if it is the right field for you.

Become technology-savvy, if you are not already, for many institutions are relying on distance-learning strategies such as online and television courses to reach their far-flung students – as well as to expand their markets.

Often promotions in the field of education mean a move out of the classroom and into administrative positions. Think this move through carefully, for those positions are often very different from classroom instruction and require different skills and abilities.

Stephen Shore advises finding a mentor at your college to help guide you through the minefield of college politics. You don't even have to tell the mentor you are on the autism spectrum if you don't want to, but build a friendship with someone you trust who will take an interest in your career and work.

One of the drawbacks of teaching for those on the autism spectrum is being able to recognize your students' faces, Shore says. "It can take a long while to get to know your students," he admits. Shore's strategies to cope with this issue include taking class roll every day and being honest with students about his problems with learning their names. Another tool would be to have students create name tents that include illustrations of their career and personal goals – in color! Then have students introduce themselves, using the name tents.

RESOURCES Definitely read *The Chronicle of Higher Education*, especially Emily Toth's "Ms. Mentor's Impeccable Advice" column. *Community Colleges Journal* is also a good source of information, as is the Association of American Colleges and Universities, 1818 R St. NW, Washington, DC 20009; www.aacu-edu.org.

For information on adult and vocational education, contact:
  ▶ Association for Career and Technical Education
    1410 King St.
    Alexandria, VA 22314
    www.acteonline.org

If teaching appeals to you, other jobs that require teaching include:
  ▶ Coaching a sports team
    (especially in a specialized sport)

  ▶ Teaching karate, yoga or other physical activity

  ▶ Teaching in a vocational or technical school where you
    teach a technical subject at which you are really good

  ▶ Teaching in a special education program

COMPUTER PROGRAMMER

Pat Brown

Computer technology has changed the way we run our
businesses, our schools, and even our personal lives. The
people who write the instructions that drive, test, and maintain software languages are computer programmers. In
addition to creating the instructions, programmers also
develop ways for computers to solve problems.

Programming is very much a niche occupation. That is,
creating instructions for the financial services industry is
very different from writing instructions for state governments to monitor school districts' progress, for example.
Compared to other computer technology jobs such as network systems analysts and computer software applications
engineers, programming will grow more slowly, from 10
percent to 20 percent between 2000 and 2010. This is mostly
due to the number of prepackaged software solutions on the
market

The 585,000 programmers in 2000 earned between
approximately $35,000 and $93,000 a year, according to the
Occupational Outlook Handbook. Computer and data processing services hired the most programmers, but you will find
a lot of programmers working for engineering, computer
and office equipment, insurance and financial services firms.
Finally, many work for temporary personnel services as the
need for programmers varies a great deal.

Pat Brown has been a programmer for more than 20 years
with an electrical utility. She has watched programming
become far more sophisticated and computers able to solve
ever more complex problems. One of the far-reaching changes
she has observed is the dot-com bust of the last few years.

"Programming just isn't as freewheeling as it used to
be," Brown notes. "People don't move around as much any
more. I don't know this for sure, but college degrees may
have become more important to employers."

In recent years, industry has become more interested in
standardized computer programs rather than creating brand
new ones. As a result, more attention is being focused on
configuring existing systems, Brown points out.

BREAKING IN When asked how you break in to the programming field, Brown advises, "This has been true forever, but don't worry about where you start, just go ahead and start. There's a good chance you'll be moving elsewhere and the technology will change in three years anyway, so get experience. Experience counts more in this field than most."

People get into programming with two-year associate's degrees, bachelor's degrees, or vocational training under their belts. Rarely, Brown says, do you see someone with a master's degree. With technology changing so quickly, such a degree may not be helpful.

SUCCESS ON THE JOB Strategies vary in this field by the specific industry in which you are using your computer skills but, in general, promotions do not happen in the way they do in other fields. People often step out on their own, starting their own programming and consulting businesses. One of the reasons for such entrepreneurship is that companies' need for programmers ebbs and flows, depending on their work load.

Programming is also one of those jobs that can be done long distance. Witness the number of American companies shifting their programming jobs overseas.

Keep up with the changes in programming languages as well as the changes in your particular niche. Be flexible and learn all you can to stay up-to-date with this fast moving field.

RESOURCES Read *PC World* and *InfoWorld* for general programming information, Brown advises, but more important, keep up with your particular industry or niche by reading related trade or professional journals.

Check out these trade and professional associations as well as those in your particular industry:

▶ IEEE Computing Society, Headquarters Office
1730 Pennsylvania Ave., NW
Washington, DC 20036-1992
www.computer.org

▶ Association for Computing Machinery (ACM)
1515 Broadway
New York, NY 10036
www.acm.org

If you are interested in computer programming, it may be best to choose jobs that are not likely to be outsourced to overseas offices. Some of them are:

▶ Computer network administrator for a large company

▶ Freelance computer specialist who solves computer problems with both hardware and software (people in these roles visit offices to fix computer problems and set up new systems)

▶ Computer programmer for a medium-sized business that is too specialized to outsource work to people overseas

▶ Computer security systems consultant

PROFESSION **DRAFTING**

> *This profile is a bit different from the others, for it involves*
> *two individuals with whom I've worked quite closely over*
> *the years, Rick Jordan and Mark Deesing. Because this is*
> *my field, I've included a few of my own comments.*

Rick Jordan
Mark Deesing

INTRODUCTION As a livestock facilities designer, I rely on drafters to take my designs and translate them onto paper. The designs have to be exact in order to work, and they have to be well drawn, whether by computer or by hand.

Two of the best drafters I know are Rick Jordan, who works for a large meat packing corporation, and Mark Deesing, who works with me at Grandin Livestock Handling Systems. Both learned to draft by hand, which, in my opinion, is the absolutely best way to get started in this field. Many companies use computer-aided drafting (CAD) programs, but often the most complex designs have to be drawn out by hand.

Drafters work for many types of organizations, all the way from architectural and aeronautical firms to oil refineries and electronic firms. Their job is to prepare the technical and specific drawings and plans for buildings, pipelines, industrial machinery, refrigerators, toys, and anything else that is manufactured or constructed. To do so, drafters use drawings, sketches and codes that instruct production or manufacturing crews in how to build the products.

Since drafters also use computer technology in their work, you have to feel comfortable with technology. In 2000, there were 213,000 people working as drafters. Forty percent of them worked for engineering and architectural firms; about 10,000 were self-employed, according to the *Occupational Outlook Handbook*. You can expect this field to grow as fast as the average for all occupations, that is, 10 percent to 20 percent between 2000 and 2010. Currently, the *Occupational Outlook Handbook* reports, drafters' salaries range from about $11.20 per hour all the way to $28.69 per hour, depending on the field in which they work as well as their experience.

Rick Jordan works as the head corporate projects designer for a large corporation specializing in the meat industry. In drafting the designs for the company's facilities and machinery, Rick acts a liaison between engineers and production crews. Rick studied drafting at a vocational college, completing the course in just one year. After he finished the program, he assisted the instructor as a student teacher of sorts and actually considered going to college to become an instructor himself.

"However, a large Colorado meat packer required a mechanical drafter and my instructor made me go for an interview to get experience in job-seeking skills. I was hired immediately after my interviewers saw my hand-drawn section of a valve," Rick admits.

Rick is not entirely sure what has helped him be successful, but he does know that as a visual thinker, he creates images as he sees them in his mind's eye – a pretty good trait for a drafter.

"I guess the key to my success has been the ability to teach myself new things and work alone," Rick says. "I have a very understanding and cooperative supervisor and the resources to research new ideas or avenues of progression, both personally and businesswise."

Mark Deesing, another drafter, has worked in the field for six years, all of that time drafting plans for livestock facilities around the world. He is excited about his work, for he has observed over the years that the meat packing industry is growing increasingly more interested in the kind of humane packing plants for which he drafts the plans.

Technology plays a large role in Mark's work. Mark uses auto-CAD and frequently e-mails designs to clients. "I can send drawings by e-mail and a lot of clients don't even require me to visit," Mark says. "I still visit some, though."

For Mark, who used to work as a farrier, shoeing horses, drafting is a wonderful opportunity to use his native creativity. Both Mark and Rick have worked on construction sites, supervising building of their designs. This in-field experience enables them to design projects that work. They also work closely with the end users of their designs to get feedback on how well the facilities worked. Feedback from people who actually use the equipment enables them to continually improve their designs.

INSIDER ADVICE

BREAKING IN For the kind of drafting he does, Mark advises spending time around animals. This is a job that benefits from such hands-on experience. Engineering skills, even if not an engineering degree, are a plus. An animal science degree would also be helpful.

Just as Rick Jordan graduated from a vocational drafting program, you should too. Technical institutes, community colleges, and some four-year colleges offer these programs, says the *Occupational Outlook Handbook*.

In high school, be sure to take math, science, computer technology, and design or computer graphics courses. Of course, you need to develop a mechanical ability and the ability to draw three-dimensional objects as well as free-hand. Finally, be sure to have some understanding of construction and manufacturing standards as well as solid problem-solving and interpersonal skills.

Both Rick and Mark learned to draw by hand before they started working with a computer. This is one reason why their drawings are so good. A person has to learn to draw before learning the computer. Trying to learn to draw at the same time you are learning the computer program is very difficult. I have received drawings from many large companies. The best drawings come from draftsmen who learned to draw by hand first. These drawings are more detailed and contain fewer mistakes.

SUCCESS ON THE JOB The American Design Drafting Association (ADDA) provides a certification program. Drafters become certified after passing the Drafter Certification Test given periodically at different sites around the country. In addition, employers want to promote those who have the strongest technical and mechanical skills. This means that you must keep up with the changes and advances in technology, as CAD allows for more versatility and range in designs.

Because drafters tend to work for industries that are cyclical, layoffs can happen more easily in this field. This means you have to do your best work and constantly improve your skills. A number of drafters work for temporary staffing agencies and may continue to work through difficult economic times.

"Don't forget," Rick Jordan says, "that the secret to success at work lies in the individual's personal pride and achievement."

Mark suggests that drafters in his field read industry publications such as *Drovers, Feedlot Magazine,* and the more academic publications *Journal of Animal Science* and *Applied Animal Behavior Science.* In addition, industry groups such as American Cattleman Association and American Association of Agricultural Consultants can provide helpful information for the livestock facilities drafting field. Whatever field you are in, you must read your industry's trade magazines.

For general information about drafting, check out:

▶ The American Design Drafting Association
P.O. Box 11937
Columbia, SC 29111
www.adda.org

Some of the places that need good design drafters include:

▶ Architects

▶ Large industrial plants of all types

▶ Building contractors of all types

▶ State highway departments

▶ City planning departments

▶ Engineering firms

PROFESSION **ENTREPRENEURSHIP**

Chris Swilley

INTRODUCTION Entrepreneurship is a growing industry in the United States. For example, in 1997, an Entrepreneurial Research Consortium study found that more than 35 million U.S. households – roughly one in three – "have had an intimate involvement in a new or small business."

According to the U.S. Small Business Administration, small firms (employing fewer than 500 individuals):

▶ Represent more than 99.7 percent of all employers

▶ Employ more than half of all private-sector employees

▶ Pay 44.5 percent of total U.S. private payroll

▶ Generate 60 to 80 percent of net new jobs annually

▶ Produce 13-14 times more patents per employee than large patenting firms (besides, these patents are twice as likely as those of large firm patents to be among the 1 percent most cited)

▶ Are employers of 39 percent of high-tech workers (such as scientists, engineers, and computer workers)

Starting a small business is an excellent way for people on the autism spectrum as it provides a way to be able to control one's work environment as much as possible. There is a way to step into entrepreneurship without becoming too overwhelmed by the responsibilities.

First, realize that you will have to become an expert on entrepreneurship before starting your business. To find a small business class in your area, check with these agencies or organizations:

▶ The U.S. Small Business Administration (www.sba.gov)

▶ The U.S. Small Business Development Centers (www.sba.gov/sbdc/)

▶ Kauffman Center for Entrepreneurial Leadership (www.entreworld.org)

▶ Association for Enterprise Opportunity (www.shoga.wwa.com/~aeo/)

▶ National Association for Community College Entrepreneurship (www.nacce.com)

Do not go into business for yourself until you have had some business training. In that training, you will learn how to research your industry, target your market and your competition, as well as gain knowledge about all the necessary parts of running a business. In addition, you will learn how to develop and understand the financial documents you will need to conduct your business.

Christine Swilley and her husband Wilson have owned several businesses in their life together, including a dog kennel and an auto repair business. In 1987, a radical management change at the meat company where Wilson worked prompted him to leave the company where he had been designing equipment.

Like most entrepreneurs, the Swilleys jumped into the business without much time to prepare, but with a great need to make a living.

"It really wasn't a dream we had to start this business. Some of it was desperation," Chris recalls. "We had been running the repair shop and kennel, which weren't doing so well. But operating those did give me the confidence to try this new business."

Thus, Bond Equipment Corporation, designer and manufacturer of heavy equipment for the meatpacking industry, was born in one bedroom of the Swilleys' home.

The Swilleys' startup experience fits the pattern for most American small-business startups. Someone in the family gets laid off from, or leaves, his or her job without much notice; a family member is sick and requires more attention; or the family needs additional income, so a home-based business gets started to solve those problems. Whatever the

INSIDER ADVICE

reason, small business entrepreneurs usually have little business training or education and even less funding for their startup.

Chris wishes that hadn't been so for her family business, but it was. Their lack of entrepreneurship training and money meant that it took longer for their business to become a healthy, profitable enterprise. But the Swilleys had a major plus going for them: Wilson had been designing machinery since 1969, so he and Chris knew the design business and the meat industry very well.

"Within eight months of Wilson starting the design business, we had 11 people working for us," Chris says.

For a small business, growth that happens too fast can be just as problematic as growth that is too slow. So what should entrepreneurs ideally know before they open their doors?

SUCCESS ON THE JOB

Chris' top what-to-know list looks like this:

▶ Know your industry and market backwards and forwards. Be focused.

▶ Be willing to learn.

▶ Develop the ability to delegate responsibilities.

▶ Be flexible, for sometimes you will have to make decisions before you have all the information you need or want.

▶ Have enough money – and then some – for undercapitalization is one of the downfalls of small businesses.

▶ Start small.

Entrepreneurship can be a good career path for people on the autism spectrum, but it can only be as successful as the planning and time you put into it. Please take the time to learn all you can, for the time you put into your business will be paid back over and over.

Types of business where an entrepreneur can be successful include:

- ▶ Graphic design and commercial art
- ▶ Niche-market computer programming in specialized areas where you do not compete with the large corporations
- ▶ Specialized equipment for different industries
- ▶ Locksmith and security systems
- ▶ Landscaping design
- ▶ Crafts such as jewelry making
- ▶ Architectural and engineering design and drafting
- ▶ Consulting, for example, developing individualized education programs for students with special needs

RESOURCES

PROFESSION **FINANCIAL ACCOUNTING AND RECORD KEEPING**

Sheryl Sunderman

INTRODUCTION

If you enjoy working with facts, figures and data, you would do well in the accounting and record keeping fields. Precision and a passion for order are what count in these occupations. For many on the autism spectrum, especially nonvisual thinkers, this kind of work can be very fulfilling.

Basically, the roles of accountants and auditors are to ensure that organizations, companies, and government entities operate efficiently and maintain good records. Bookkeepers and accounting clerks, on the other hand, do the actual recording of financial data for a wide variety of organizations and businesses. However, the accounting field is broadening to include budget analysis, information technology consulting, and even financial and investment planning. According to the 2002-2003 *Occupational Outlook Handbook,* this means that accountants must come into the field with an even wider scope of abilities and skills. The same advice is good for bookkeepers as well, because the more experience and skills you have, the easier it will be to be hired.

Jobs for accountants and auditors are expected to increase between 10-20 percent through the year 2010, about average for all occupations, according to the *Occupational Outlook Handbook*. In 2000, median annual earnings for the 976,000 accountants and auditors in the United States were $43,500.

The number of jobs for bookkeepers and accounting clerks is expected to increase by only 0-2 percent in the same time period. Why? Organizations are using improved technology and are consolidating record keeping tasks, so there are fewer openings. But this is such a huge field – approximately 2 million people worked in 2000 as bookkeepers and accounting clerks in the United States – that even if it is not a growing profession, there will still be lots of jobs as people leave their jobs or become promoted. However, many of those positions will be for temporary employment agencies as many organizations now outsource these kinds of record keeping jobs. Also note that in the financial services industry, many of these data-driven jobs are being sent overseas where the costs of doing business are lower than in the United States.

Sheryl Sunderman, a certified public accountant, advises people interested in accounting to not only master the necessary financial skills but the communicative skills as well. Clear verbal and written communication is key for doing well in this competitive business. It is also good practice to know as much as possible about information technology because accounting firms often consult with clients about their technology needs. At a minimum, be very good at using Microsoft Word and Excel programs, the workhorses of the office.

Although the stereotype of the lonely accountant, head bent, shoulders slumped, poring over financial documents is still partially true, at least some of the work day, Sunderman points out that accountants must also have good people skills. Accountants spend part of their time in meetings with clients and colleagues, and teamwork skills are essential for a thriving practice as well.

This is a good time for women to enter the field, Sunderman says; indeed, more women are currently enrolled in accounting college programs than men.

INSIDER ADVICE

Most accounting jobs require at least a bachelor's degree in accounting or a related field. Some employers want their staff members to have a master's degree in accounting or business administration with an emphasis on accounting. All partners in an accounting firm must be licensed by the state in which they work.

Enrollment is down in college accounting programs, in general, so accounting firms are visiting college campuses to recruit and build their ranks. If this is a field that interests you, and for which you seem to have the requisite skills and talents, visit with them and build a relationship early on with the accounting firms in your area. Accounting is now a five-year degree program, so plan to spend additional time in college, but also work toward landing an internship, a great way to get work experience. In addition, start taking bookkeeping and accounting classes in high school. That is how Sunderman started in the business, and this helped her shape her career plan early on. You might even work as a bookkeeper or records clerk while working toward your accounting degree. It is a great way to learn about the business in general.

BREAKING IN

SUCCESS ON THE JOB

Sunderman's advice to accountants wishing to be promoted is pretty simple:

▶ Take and pass the certified public accountant exam. To be a candidate for that exam in most states, you must complete 150 college credit hours – 30 more than what is necessary for a typical four-year bachelor's degree. That step is very important toward advancing in the field; but it requires discipline and additional time studying.

▶ Be willing to work overtime.

▶ Be able to "multitask" – do several things at once.

▶ Keep up-to-date on changes in accounting practice and standards.

▶ Make your deadlines!

As businesses and other organizations become more "accounting savvy," Sunderman says, so must the accountants who serve them. "Try to learn as much as you can," she advises.

The accounting profession is flexible enough to include several different career paths. The four major fields of accounting are as follows:

▶ **Public accountants** – perform a broad range of services, including accounting, auditing, tax preparation, and consulting for a wide variety of clients. They may specialize in taxes, compensation and health-care benefits, and even forensic accounting in bankruptcy cases.

▶ **Management accountants** – also work for a wide variety of clients but perform executive functions such as budgeting, performance evaluation, and cost-and-asset management. They are usually part of executive teams involved in strategic planning or new product development.

► **Government accountants and auditors** – ensure that government agencies and organizations doing business with them follow the law in financial reporting and expenditures.

► **Internal auditors** – verify that organizations have spent their monies in a proper manner and check for waste and fraud.

Sunderman recommends reading *The Journal of Accountancy* and *Accounting Journal* and keeping up with any changing state or professional standards for financial reporting.

In addition, there are a number of professional associations for accountants. This includes the following:

RESOURCES

► Institute of Management Accountants
10 Paragon Dr.
Montvale, NJ 07645-1760
www.imanet.org

► The Institute of Internal Auditors
249 Maitland Ave.
Altamonte Springs, FL 32701-4201
www.theiia.org

For more information on bookkeeping and accounting clerk careers, contact:

► The American Institute of
Professional Bookkeepers
6001 Montrose Rd.
Rockville, MD 20852
www.aipb.org

If accounting appeals to you, you may also be interested in other financial jobs such as

► Stocks and bonds analyst
► Government budget analyst
► Government statistician
► Internal Revenue Services agent

PROFESSION **GRAPHIC ARTS DESIGN**

Kim Tappan

INTRODUCTION   For those with a strong visual sense and a creative drive, graphic design can be an interesting and fulfilling career. Graphic designers work for a variety of organizations creating print and electronic designs. Using computer software, graphic designers create designs and layout for magazines, newspapers, journals, corporate reports, and other publications. They also create designs for advertising and promotional displays, marketing brochures, company logos, Internet web pages and more.

Graphic design is a very healthy field thanks to the growing need for web-based designs and the growth of video productions, the *2003 Occupational Outlook Handbook* reports. The field will have a faster-than-average growth rate through 2010. In 2000, median annual earnings were $34,570.

This is also a career path full of entrepreneurs, such as Kim Tappan, owner of Tappan Design.

INSIDER ADVICE   Tappan has been working as a graphic designer since graduating with a bachelor's and master's degree in fine arts. "I didn't want to be a starving artist," Tappan laughs, "so I taught art at the college for a while after graduation."

Later Tappan went to work for a printing company's art department, where she learned as much as she could as fast as she could. That, in fact, is her first piece of advice: Try everything in order to learn the business.

This can-do attitude worked well for Tappan, who, after the company shut down its art department, bought its equipment and opened her own design firm using the very skills she learned at the printing company.

In her nearly 20 years in the field, Tappan has watched graphic designs become more high-tech and complex – as well as more competitive – thanks partly to the increasing number of home computers and software programs. Tappan does not try to compete with home-based designers; instead, she focuses on larger, more complex design jobs such as book design.

She also has watched the field become more entrepreneurial as more and more graphic designers open up their own firms. They have had plenty of business, Tappan explains, as small specialty advertising and marketing firms have gone to hiring outside designers for projects. At the same time, larger organizations have downsized or disbanded their in-house design departments, so they too have hired outside designers for projects.

Keeping up with the changes is critical, whether it's new font designs or new pricing standards. Tappan suggests joining the American Institute of Graphic Arts and the Printing Industry of America, two trade associations whose conferences and publications help her keep up with the business. Tappan also attends the yearly HOW Conference and reads its publication, *HOW Magazine*.

If you are going to own a business, Tappan says, you have to be able to sell your work, so networking and good social skills are a must. If they aren't your strengths, make sure you have someone working with you who can handle that part of the business.

BREAKING IN

Learn, learn, learn as much as you can, Tappan advises. If you are in college, make sure you get an internship. Design theory is good to have, but working experience is the best teacher, so go to work – even if you have to work for free in the beginning. Learn all you can about computer programs, but make sure you have a practiced eye for good design.

"I see a lot of really talented kids coming out of college, but they don't have good design skills," Tappan points out. "You need to have a good eye for layout and design. I benefited from my fine arts background. It's all about design. I would suggest they take fine arts courses to improve their design. They have mastered a lot of techniques like Photoshop, but how it gets laid out on the page is what makes or breaks the design."

Yet, it is still a good idea to have a college degree, whether it's a bachelor of arts or a two-year associate's degree from a community college. Attending a trade school would be good, too, Tappan adds. But make sure you learn more than just the basics. If you can, get a background in the printing process.

SUCCESS ON THE JOB

Being a good designer is one thing, but building relationships is also important for being successful in the graphic arts design field. Even if you are not self-employed, you still have to have good enough social skills to communicate with clients and colleagues. They are entrusting you with their work, and they want to know you can handle the job, so develop your social skills as much as you can so clients and employers will have faith in you. Always try different jobs in a company to make yourself more indispensable.

The *Occupational Outlook Handbook* advises designers to not only be flexible and open to new ideas, but to be well read and able to react to changing trends. Good problem-solving skills are important, and so is the ability to work independently and to meet deadlines.

RESOURCES

▶ *Print Magazine*

▶ *Communication Arts*

▶ *HOW Magazine*

For information about graphic design careers, contact:

▶ American Institute of Graphic Arts
164 Fifth Ave.
New York, NY 10010
www.aiga.org

Other occupations that use similar skills as graphic design include:

▶ Architectural and engineering drafting
▶ Still photography
▶ Video photography (film, movies or TV)

HVAC (HEATING, VENTILATION, AIR CONDITIONING)

Don West

If you were one of those kids who took the family toaster and
radio apart any chance you got, then working in the heating,
air conditioning and refrigeration field might be for you. It is an
extremely healthy field, growing faster than the average profession, between 21 and 35 percent per year, through 2010.

It is not hard to understand why there is such growth in
this occupation. Air conditioning and heating systems are
everywhere – homes, schools, office buildings, factories, gro-
ceries, clothing stores, and other businesses. As the world
has grown "smaller" and more connected, these once luxu-
ries of modern living have spread far and wide, and so has
the need for qualified professionals to install, maintain and
repair these increasingly more complex systems, which
include mechanical, electrical and electronic components.
Although trained to do both heating and cooling, technicians often specialize in installation, maintenance or repair
of one type of equipment.

In 2000, the more than 243,000 heating, air conditioning
and refrigeration technicians in the United States earned a
median wage of $15.76 per hour. About one third of those
worked for cooling and heating contractors, the remainder
were employed by a variety of industries and governments,
reports the *Occupational Outlook Handbook*. About one in five
were self-employed, like Don West.

Don and his son Bryan do it all. They install, maintain, and
repair heating and air conditioning systems in homes and businesses. A former railroad engineer, Don left his job with the
railroad when that industry started to look shaky and went to
school to learn HVAC. He learned it so well that he now teaches the subject as adjunct faculty at a community college.

In recent years, Don says, a major trend in the HVAC
industry has been for large corporations to buy and then
consolidate many small and medium-sized heating and
cooling companies into larger ones. This enables them to set
prices, driving some small mom-and-pop operations out of
business. At the same time, Don notes, there are not enough
qualified technicians working in the field.

BREAKING IN Although no formal education is required to enter this field, most companies want their employees to have some prior training, whether from on-the-job experience or a trade school or local college program. To learn about the industry, be sure to join and attend meetings of various trade organizations. Also visit with owners of small HVAC companies and see if they would be willing to offer an internship. Expect to start at the bottom and show a willingness to progress.

"I've seen too many students graduate from a program think that they should be able to immediately start earning top pay," Don says. "In reality, they are merely ready to start the learning process."

More and more cities are requiring some kind of certification of technicians working in the field. Also, in order to start a business and obtain a business license, one must be certified as a master by a nationally recognized testing organization.

SUCCESS ON THE JOB You get promoted in this business usually by showing an interest in your work and gaining more knowledge by attending seminars and training sessions, Don says.

One of the changes going on in this field right now is the growing complexity of the HVAC equipment and systems. For instance, notes the *Occupational Outlook Handbook*, HVAC technicians are able to use a new technology, a form of cellular "web" phone that enables them to access the Internet from the field while diagnosing equipment problems. In addition, computer hardware and software now allow heating and air conditioning equipment to automatically notify the maintenance department when problems arise. This means that HVAC technicians must be very familiar with computer technology in order to do their job well.

RESOURCES Several trade organizations provide information about the HVAC industry, including:

▶ Air-Conditioning Contractors of America (ACCA)
2800 Shirlington Rd., Suite 300
Arlington, VA 22206
www.acca.org

▶ Refrigeration Service Engineers Society (RSES)
1666 Rand Rd.
Des Plaines, IL 60016-3552

▶ National Association of Plumbing-Heating-
Cooling Contractors (PHCC)
180 S. Washington St.
P.O. Box 6808
Falls Church, VA 22046
www.naphcc.org

Other jobs that use similar skills include:

▶ Auto mechanic
▶ Industrial maintenance staff
(repairs factory equipment)
▶ Electrician
▶ Plumber

PROFESSION **INFORMATION TECHNOLOGY**

Monica Johnston

INTRODUCTION Those born with a curious mind and a tinker's nature may want to try a job repairing the equipment that makes our work – and personal lives – easier. Repairing computers, office machinery, and even automated teller machines could be a great way to find satisfying employment in these changeable times.

Banks cannot operate without automated tellers, grocery stores don't run if their cash register breaks down, and schools and offices would be at a loss without photocopiers. Given our need for these important machines, we are in debt to the people who show up, repair them, and then leave so we can get back to the business of the day.

These jobs are stable, and given the mobility of today's economy, that is a good thing. As long as there are offices, schools, stores, assembly lines, banks, government agencies, and other organizations at work, somebody has to fix the machines when they break. That somebody might as well be you.

In 2000, 172,000 people in America made their living fixing broken computers, office machines and automated teller machines. They made between $11.80 and $23.42 per hour, notes the *2002-2003 Occupational Outlook Handbook*. This field is expected to grow between 10 and 20 percent from 2000 to 2010.

INSIDER ADVICE Monica Johnston teaches her students how to use computers as well as repair them at her community college in the Midwest. She started graduate school with a different major, but ended up switching after an "aha" moment in one of her college courses.

"I took a required Introduction to Information Technology class in graduate school," Johnston recalls. "The instructor was enthusiastic about computers and technology and her excitement was contagious. By the second or third week of class, I changed my degree emphasis and my career plans."

Many of Johnston's students at the community college are changing careers or starting all over, so her own experience is valuable for her students. She emphasizes that the information technology field has changed greatly over the last decade. For example, it is hard to overstate the influence the Internet has had on business and society in general. The ability to connect to customers creates many opportunities for businesses. However, the Internet is not a panacea. Businesses and individuals lost millions of dollars investing in fledgling "dot-com" ventures in the mid- to late 1990s. The businesses that survived the fallout are now trying to regroup and realistically evaluate the opportunities and challenges created by technology.

"My advice is to be flexible," Johnston says, "for technology changes so rapidly. You have to be ready to respond to these changes and adapt to be successful." Second, she adds, you must commit to a lifetime of training and learning to keep up with the changes in technology.

BREAKING IN

In addition, you need strong analytical and critical thinking skills. Technical education often does not emphasize communication and interpersonal skills, but these are essential to be successful. Professionals are required to obtain industry-recognized certifications, as well as traditional education and training.

In general, a strong foundation in electronics is necessary to repair computers, office machinery, and automated teller machines. Employers want you to be certified as repairers and have training from associate degree programs, the military, vocational schools, or equipment manufacturers, according to the *2002-2003 Occupational Outlook Handbook*. Several professional and trade organizations offer certification programs for electronic or computer equipment repairers. Being certified means you have passed several tests assessing your repair skills, which makes you more valuable to an employer.

The opportunity for promotion varies greatly in the computer repair field. The size of the organization often determines the opportunities for advancement, whether technical or management.

SUCCESS ON THE JOB

Experience and the ability to keep up with technical changes in equipment will help individuals become promoted. Employers often pay for additional training. The more training you get and the more equipment you know how to repair, the better your chances of advancing in this field.

RESOURCES   The *2002-2003 Occupational Outlook Handbook* web site lists these resources for the computer, office machinery, and automated teller repair fields:

▶ Computing Technology Industry Association
450 East 22nd St., Suite 230
Lombard, IL 60148-6158
www.comptia.org

▶ International Society of Certified
Electronics Technicians
3608 Pershing Ave.
Fort Worth, TX 76107
www.iscet.org

▶ Electronics Technicians Association
502 North Jackson
Greencastle, IN 46135

Other jobs that use computer skills include:
▶ Computer network administrator in a large office
▶ Repair person for ATM bank machines
▶ Computer troubleshooter
▶ Computer setup technician who helps people install new software or hardware
▶ Repair person for computerized inventory systems in large stores
▶ Telecommunications and telephone network specialist

LEARNING SPECIALIST

PROFESSION

Denise Zortman

Educational services, one of the biggest fields in the United States today, includes learning specialists and tutor positions, two very important jobs in colleges and universities. These individuals work with students of all capabilities in a wide variety of settings. Sometimes the additional assistance offered by a learning specialist can mean the difference between passing and failing for a student.

INTRODUCTION

Look for learning specialists and tutors in college teaching/learning centers, English-as-Second Language programs, counseling centers, special education programs, and government-sponsored programs for first-generation college students.

Denise Zortman coordinates the learning resources program at a community college in the Midwest.

INSIDER ADVICE

"The most important trend I have observed is a lack of student preparedness for college," Zortman says. "Colleges today are teaching more students with developmental needs as well as a lot of adults who are returning to school."

Social issues affect this field as well. For example, welfare-to-work legislation has forced many to seek job training and education. If students have not been in school for a while, they often need this kind of special assistance to learn how to be successful in college. Also, students with various kinds of mild disabilities are enrolling in two- and four-year colleges in increasing numbers as legislation in recent years has mandated supports and accommodations making it easier for students with disabilities to successfully attend postsecondary institutions.

The best way to get hired as a learning specialist is to work as a tutor while in college, Zortman advises. It's a great job for a college student, she adds, for research shows that teaching someone also helps the learner master the subject. You must have at least a bachelor's degree to work as a learning specialist, but many have master's degrees. You might also consider completing a tutor certification program that some professional associations offer, such as the College Reading and Learning Association.

BREAKING IN

SUCCESS ON THE JOB

Because you are working with students of varying abilities, you have to be very flexible. For example, at one table, you may be tutoring addition problems and at the next table you're showing a student how to work differential equations. Develop as many learning strategies as you can, Zortman advises, because everyone learns differently.

With the emphasis on clear writing, learning specialists should have strong writing skills, as many students need help in this area. Even if your job is to tutor math, you can often use writing in coaching students on a variety of subjects. The lack of student preparation is not only affecting community colleges but four-year institutions as well. So, Zortman says, those schools are also offering tutoring programs.

Promotion in this field generally means you become an assistant director or director of a learning center. Sometimes you can even end up working as a college instructor. To be really successful in this very important job, you must work with the "whole" student. That is, you need to take into consideration students' learning styles, their personal and emotional lives, etc.

RESOURCES

▶ College Reading and Learning Association, CRLA
P.O. Box 6251
Auburn, CA 95604
www.crla.net

▶ National Center for Developmental Education
Reich College of Education
Appalachian State University
Boone, NC 28608
ncde.appstate.edu

▶ National Association for Developmental
Education (NADE)
2447 Tiffin Ave., #207
Findlay, OH 45840
nade.net

Other jobs that use similar skills include:

▶ Special education teacher

▶ Occupational therapist

▶ Speech therapist

LIBRARY JOBS

Gloria Maxwell

Libraries are wonderful places to work. They are quiet, but there is always a lot to do. There are books for browsing, magazines for reading, and technology for exploring the world.

There were 149,000 people working as librarians in 2000, most of them in school and academic libraries, according to the *Occupational Outlook Handbook.* A smaller number worked for governments, hospitals, religious organizations, and businesses of various kinds. Salaries vary, depending on qualifications and the size, type, and location of the library. In general, though, yearly salaries ranged from less than $25,000 to approximately $63,000 and above.

Sadly, the *Occupational Outlook Handbook* states that this is a slow-growing field, partly due to the increasing use of computerized systems for cataloging, storing and retrieving information. And with the public accessing library research materials from their own home computers, fewer people are needed behind the reference desk.

You don't have to be a reference librarian with a master's degree in library science to work in a library. Library technicians do everything from checking out books, to repairing books, inputting information into computer systems, preparing invoices, handling media equipment, and assisting patrons. If you work in a small library, count on doing just about everything; those who work in larger, urban libraries may get to specialize.

In 2000, some 109,000 library technicians worked in school, academic and public libraries as well as government agencies. A high school diploma is usually necessary for this job, although some technician jobs require a two-year degree or even a bachelor's. And like many other jobs these days, having computer skills is a must. This occupation is expected to grow faster than average, between 10 and 20 percent, from 2000 and 2010. But libraries have been hit hard by the poor economy and that could slow growth. Salary ranges from a low of just under $14,000 to more than $36,000 per year. Those working for college and university libraries earned the most while elementary and secondary school technicians earned the least.

Librarians don't just work in libraries these days. You will find them organizing data for companies, creating databases and reference tools, as well as consulting with organizations about their information systems.

The biggest change librarian Gloria Maxwell has seen in her field can be summed up in one word: technology! "I think when libraries first started adopting technology, we were suspicious of it," Maxwell recalls. "But librarians need to understand the technology or they will be left behind."

That technology also has opened up new – and sometimes raging – debates over freedom of information. For librarians, access to information is extremely important, but offering Internet services in the library has made that access a dilemma at times. "Librarians have always supported freedom of information," Maxwell says. "And when librarians select a book, it is a choice. But the Internet brings in all sorts of information to libraries that have not been selected. Yet, public libraries still don't want to filter information."

One of the important jobs librarians do these days is teach people how to differentiate between good and bad information, reliable from unreliable. Strong communication skills are necessary for this particular library position as well as flexibility. So if you want to be a reference librarian, develop your communication skills for teaching and demonstrating are key parts of a librarian's daily work.

For those who love to count and work more on their own, Maxwell suggests working in the cataloging and indexing departments of a library. If you love detail work, she says, you will love the rule and guide books catalogers and indexers use in their work.

The best way to find out if you would like library work is to work in one, Maxwell advises. Work as a library technician, shelve books while you're in high school, or help staff the circulation desk. That way you will know a lot about what you like and dislike about library work early on.

Once you have decided you like it, you'll need to earn a master's degree in library science in order to work as a reference librarian. If you like the sciences, you have a real edge, for there is a shortage of librarians with a science background, she says.

Whatever your interest, unless you have a library science degree from an American Library Association accredited program, you won't get an interview. Maxwell's advice is to earn an undergraduate degree in a field that interests you and then get a master's degree in library science. An undergraduate degree in library science will not get you the job.

Look outside traditional library jobs for employment, including information brokers, private corporations, and consulting firms. Your research, organizational skills and knowledge of computer databases are very much needed by these organizations.

SUCCESS ON THE JOB

Experience counts here, for as quiet as they may be, libraries are busy places and need reliable staff members who are versatile and flexible. If you want to work at a four-year college library, Maxwell advises getting a double master's degree to help you specialize in a field of your interest.

If you work at a small library, where many of the job openings are in the library field, you need to be able to handle as many tasks as possible. Most people flock to big-city libraries for jobs, but the jobs for the next few years are in small towns and rural areas. Plan ahead for this by getting as much and as varied experience as you can.

RESOURCES

▶ American Library Association
50 East Huron St.
Chicago, IL 60611
www.ala.org

States have their own library membership and professional associations. Maxwell suggests reading the following professional journals:

▶ *American Libraries*
▶ *Library Journal*
▶ *School Library Journal*
▶ *Academic College and Research Libraries (ACRL)*

Other jobs that use similar skills are:

▶ Journalist (I have met many journalists who work for either newspapers or TV who may be on the spectrum. They have developed a reputation for being good in specialized areas such as science, education or politics.)
▶ Accountant
▶ Financial specialist
▶ Government statistician who monitors markets such as grain or steel

129

PROFESSION **PRINTING**

Senta Cisneros

INTRODUCTION One of the most varied industries in the nation has to be printing and publishing. The 1.5 million Americans working in that industry perform a wide range of jobs as they scramble to get newspapers out on time, postcards delivered to vacation resorts, memo pads trimmed properly, and bank checks printed with correct account numbers. Nearly 70 percent work for either commercial printing establishments or newspapers.

Although printing is one of the nation's largest manufacturers, most printing businesses are small, employing fewer than 10 people. This is an industry that is geographically widespread, with printing plants located throughout the country.

Because the jobs are so different, there is no one median earnings figure for this field. As for growth in this broad industry, in general, it is declining slightly but certain jobs such as desktop publishing and magazine and journal printing are growing rapidly.

INSIDER ADVICE For client services manager Senta Cisneros, the work day is fast-paced and full of deadlines. She talks with a lot of people and does whatever she needs to get a customer's printing job completed and out the door on time. By its nature, printing can be stressful, with a lot of deadlines. It is very "client-focused," relies heavily on computer technology, and staff members work together as a team. In general, the smaller the shop, Cisneros says, the more jobs staff members are expected to handle.

However, there are also less stressful positions in printing companies. And although they too must meet the always-present deadlines of a print shop, these employees may have less stress on the job because they don't have to work directly with customers. Some of these jobs include:

> ▶ **Printing press operators** – prepare, maintain, and operate the different types of printing presses. Their duties vary depending on the type of printing press

> ▶ **Photocopy machine operators** – operate and maintain the increasingly more complex photocopy machines

▶ **Graphics specialists** – use computers to design graphics for customers' printing jobs

▶ **Bindery machine operators** – operate the machinery that combines the printed sheets into the customers' orders, whether it is books, magazines, catalogues, folders, packaging or a wide variety of other printed products

BREAKING IN

Depending on the job, you may enter this field by getting some vocational training as well as on-the-job training, Cisneros says. In general, you should have a high school degree with good mathematical, verbal and written communication skills. Definitely be computer literate and be willing to learn more about technology as you continue to work for an organization. Attitude is extremely important and so is a strong work ethic. This is a business that requires flexibility and a willingness to pitch in.

SUCCESS ON THE JOB

Because of it dependence on technology, the printing business needs people to stay on top of changes. "The more you know, the more valuable you are in this business," Cisneros says. The more you can juggle, the better off you will be. "The most important thing in this business is change, training and attitude," she adds.

RESOURCES

For more information on the printing industry, contact one of these organizations:

▶ Bindery Industries Association
70 East Lake St., #300
Chicago, IL 60601

▶ Graphic Communications Council
1899 Preston White Dr.
Reston, VA 20191
www.npes.org/edcouncil/

▶ Graphic Arts Technical Foundation
200 Deer Run Rd.
Sewickley, PA 15143
www.gatf.org

- ▶ Graphic Communications International Union
  1900 L St. NW
  Washington, DC 20036
  www.gciu.org

- ▶ National Association of Printers and
  Lithographers
  75 W. Century Rd.
  Paramus, NJ 07652
  www.napl.org

- ▶ Printing Industries of America
  100 Daingerfield Rd.
  Alexandria, VA 22314
  www.gain.org/servlet/gateway/PIA_GATF/non_
  index.html

Other jobs with similar requirements include the following:

- ▶ Bindery worker
- ▶ Graphic designer
- ▶ Advertising salesperson

BIOLOGICAL AND MEDICAL RESEARCH SCIENTIST

Ron Jenkins

Type in the job category "scientist," and the online *Occupational Outlook Handbook* responds with 12 categories, all the way from "biological and medical scientist" to "federal government." Clearly, whatever your interest, there's a scientist somewhere at work researching it.

That's the good news about this profession. You get to spend time working with scientific ideas, problems and questions that fascinate you. That by itself is a piece of luck. The bad news, though, is that, depending on the particular field, the competition for research scientist positions can be intense. So you'll want to spend some time in the library researching the opportunities and then talk with those working in the field itself.

Now, having said that, there's probably no more rewarding – and interesting – work than being able to spend time studying the scientific questions and principles you find fascinating. For this section, we're looking at the broad category of "biological and medical scientists" and the work they do for research institutions. You will find the 138,000 scientists employed in this field in 2000 working for a variety of local, state and federal government agencies, pharmaceutical companies, biotechnology organizations, hospitals, research and testing laboratories, and educational institutions.

The median annual salary for biological scientists in 2000 was $49,239 and $57,196 for medical scientists, according to the *Occupational Outlook Handbook*. And although this job category is expected to grow faster than the average for all occupations between 2000 and 2010, those holding doctoral degrees will face stiff competition. Those holding undergraduate or master's degrees in the biological sciences will have an easier time finding science-related jobs in sales, marketing and management positions due to their content knowledge.

Biochemist Ron Jenkins followed his interest in health and fitness into a research job studying genetically modified grains for the United States Department of Agriculture. We will let him tell his own story:

"During the late 1970s, people were becoming more health conscious with regard to eating 'natural' foods and also avoiding foods containing additives and preservatives. I read the labels on food products and could not pronounce them. I thought it would be great to understand why these 'chemicals' are being put into foods, and questioned whether they have a deleterious effect on human health. Red dye no. 2 was taken off the market and nitrosamines were considered as high risk for cancer. So I decided to pursue a 'nutritional science' degree from the University of Florida.

Once I obtained my B.S. degree in nutrition, I was working as a county health inspector. While there were challenges and responsibilities in this position, my true desire was to work in the laboratory, trying to understand disease processes. I knew that I would need more education beyond a B.S. in nutrition. Thus, I completed a B.S. in chemistry with the intentions of going on to graduate school to pursue a Ph.D. in biochemistry.

While working as a graduate student and postdoctoral fellow, I used a molecular biology approach to understand human disease processes in such diverse fields as cancer, immunology, toxicology and related disease. I learned a technique called 'polymerase chain reaction' and used it for several of my research projects. The United States Department of Agriculture needed a person with my background to assist in developing methods to detect the presence of genetically modified events in grains, such as corn and oilseeds. This is the type of research that I am doing today."

Careers don't always follow a straight, or even clear-cut, path, so it's important to know how your skills and abilities can be transferred to different job situations. In Jenkins' case, his use of the "polymerase chain reaction" (PCR) technique in human disease research opened doors for him at the United States Department of Agriculture because it was interested in using that PCR technique in its work with genetically modified plants (GMOs).

BREAKING IN You must have a strong science background, with a graduate degree preferred. You also need to have good computer and communication skills, Jenkins adds.

There are both science and non-science issues that need to be resolved in this industry. You have to be both a good scientist and a good politician. People who go into science must be patient, persistent and goal oriented. It can be one of the most rewarding professions for those who stay focused, work hard and persevere.

You have to be able to work independently as well as part of a team. If you are interested in working in private industry, you most demonstrate strong business skills and an understanding of regulatory issues. If you will be doing research in far-away places, you must have physical stamina.

Research scientists usually spend time in a postdoctoral job where they are able to obtain valuable laboratory experience. Sometimes those positions can lead to a permanent job.

In terms of promotions, the federal government employs specialists who review each position's potential promotion, Jenkins points out. These positions are advertised and are available at the USAJOBS website. Generally speaking, the higher your degree, the greater your promotion potential.

People researching GMOs generally belong to one or more of the following organizations:

▶ Association of Analytical Chemists (AOAC), www.aoac.org

▶ American Oil Chemists Society (AOCS), www.aocs.org

▶ American Association for the Advancement of Science (AAAS), www.aaas.org

▶ American Association of Cereal Chemists (AACC), www.aaccnet.org

▶ International Seed Testing Association, www.seedtest.org

▶ All of these organizations contain peer-reviewed publications in their journals.

For information on careers in biochemistry or biological sciences, contact:

▶ Federation of American Societies for
Experimental Biology
9650 Rockville Pike
Bethesda, MD 20814
www.faseb.org

SUCCESS ON THE JOB

RESOURCES

PROFESSION **LANGUAGE INTERPRETER/TRANSLATOR**

Gloria Donohue-Little

INTRODUCTION Do you like to pore over maps and read *National Geographic Magazine*? Is memorizing state capitals and city populations one of your favorite pastimes? If you can say yes to those questions, think about becoming a language translator and interpreter.

Our world is opening up, and international travel and business are much more feasible than just 10 years ago. Technology is creating bridges between nations and people that a few years ago had little to do with each other.

As the world's economy grows more global, more international, there is a greater need for people who can translate documents and interpret for meetings and other events. Companies are crossing borders, operating offices and plants in countries across the globe.

The 20,000 or more language translators and interpreters in the United States have the very important job of making sure we all understand each other well enough to make sure a hospital patient who doesn't speak English gets proper care, that contracts between businesses and their multinational vendors are understood by both sides, and that recently arrived immigrants have their paperwork filled out correctly. Although this is a small field, it is a highly important one for our increasingly multinational world. That is why the *Occupational Outlook Handbook* lists language translation and interpretation as one of the career paths that are growing faster than the average occupation.

INSIDER ADVICE Gloria J. Donohue-Little has 40 years of experience in this field and started her translation business 12 years ago. A native of La Pas, Bolivia, Donohue-Little grew up fascinated by all the different languages she heard spoken around her as a child.

Her company translates documents of all sorts into foreign languages as well as into English. The biggest change she has seen in the translation field is the many different ways her clients can now communicate with each other. From express mail to faxes to Internet and software programs, communication has changed and adopted many forms over the years. The speed of these communication forms makes for a more demanding schedule for translators and interpreters.

There's a big difference between being bilingual and being a translator, Donohue-Little points out. "Most of our translators travel to their country once or twice a year to immerse themselves in the culture and stay up-to-date," she explains. "These visits help them develop the cultural nuances that are terribly important to doing a good job of translating."

To get started as a translator/interpreter, first develop a passion for different cultures and languages. Even developing a deep interest in just one language will help you step into this very interesting business. "Become an expert in that language," Donohue-Little says.

Get training from a university or college and be sure to keep up on the changes occurring in the languages you translate or interpret. Language changes and grows with the country or culture, and to be an effective translator, you must move with it.

A master's degree in the language would be helpful, but Donohue-Little also contracts out to a number of retired professionals – scientists, doctors, engineers and lawyers – for their expertise in their particular field as well as their ability with the language.

Although Donohue-Little employs primarily independent contractors for her translation business, some translators work for companies and organizations. However, the majority are independent contractors with multiple clients. She advises people to become certified and accredited by the American Translators Association as a way to show ability and skills. This field requires great attention to detail and changes in the language and culture.

▶ American Translators Association
225 Reinekers Lane, Ste. 590
Alexandria, VA 22314
www.atanet.org

Other jobs that use similar skills:
▶ Tour guide
▶ Editor
▶ Magazine writer

BREAKING IN

SUCCESS ON THE JOB

RESOURCES

PROFESSION **VETERINARY ASSISTANT AND TECHNICIAN**

Jane Jeffries

INTRODUCTION I have had a special love of animals all my life. I spent a lot of time around animals as I was growing up, showing horses at 4-H fairs, helping my aunt with her livestock on her ranch. I don't think I am unusual in my love of animals and feel that many of us on the autism spectrum are attuned to their ways. That is why working as a veterinary technician or assistant is such a great job for many of us.

Veterinary assistants provide basic care for the animals being treated in the clinic. In the course of a day, you will find assistants feeding, watering, bathing, and exercising the animals under their care. In addition, they may clean, repair and disinfect cages as well as provide companionship for animals.

Most of the 145,000 people working in the animal care field in 2000 worked for kennels, veterinary clinics, animal hospitals, stables and shelters. Unfortunately, the salary is not great, ranging between $5.75 and $12.70 an hour in 2000, according to the *Occupational Outlook Handbook.*

Technicians assist veterinarians with medical treatments, including bandaging, teeth cleaning, installing IV catheters and monitoring anesthesia. In the course of their day, technicians may also perform lab tests, prepare vaccines, take blood samples, maintain equipment and a host of other tasks.

Both technicians and animal care assistant jobs are growing faster than the average for all occupations from 2000-2010, approximately 21 to 35 percent. The *Occupational Outlook Handbook* did not list salary range for animal care assistants.

INSIDER ADVICE Jane Jeffries has a small animal veterinary practice in the Midwest. To do this kind of work, you have to love animals, of course, but you have to appreciate the people who come with them too, Jeffries says. Being curious doesn't hurt either. "Medicine is sort of like detective work," Jeffries points out. "There's always something new and interesting."

Although animal care is fulfilling work, it can be difficult, both emotionally and physically. You need to be able to protect yourself from the emotional ups and downs that can come with treating ill animals. Develop some kind of system for handling the distress of caring for animals that are in pain, or worse, dying.

First, have animals at home while you're young. There's nothing like growing up around a menagerie of different animals to teach you how to take care of them. The experience is invaluable. Work in a veterinary clinic or hospital; you can even volunteer, suggests Jeffries. Get that hands-on experience.

"Be certain of your choice before spending the college time," she says. Once you do know this is your career choice, take the necessary undergraduate requirements in college before signing up for a veterinarian technician program, usually offered at community colleges.

BREAKING IN

Promotion in this field depends on the type of employer with whom you work. Animal care workers at kennels and animal shelters may choose to take the American Boarding Kennels Association home-study program to work toward becoming a Certified Kennel Operator. If you work in an animal shelter, you may take training programs and workshops through the Humane Society of the United States, the American Humane Association, and the National Animal Control Association.

Because veterinary clinics and hospitals tend to be smaller organizations, there is often less opportunity for advancement other than working towards becoming an office manager. That comes with experience, education and proven skill on the job.

SUCCESS ON THE JOB

Read industry journals such as *Veterinary Forum, The American Veterinary Medical Association Journal* and *Compendium for Continuing Education.*

RESOURCES

▶ The Humane Society of the United States
2100 L St. NW
Washington, DC 20037-1598
www.hsus.org

Other jobs that use similar skills are:
▶ Physician
▶ Chiropractor
▶ Podiatrist
▶ Research scientist

References

Introduction

Clark, R. W. (1971). *Einstein: The life and times*. New York: Thomas Y. Crowell.

Grandin, T. (1995). *Thinking in pictures and other reports from my life with autism*. New York: Vintage Books.

Grant, V. W. (1968). *Great abnormals*. New York: Hawthorn.

Kevin, G. (1967). *Inspired amateurs*. Freeport, New York: Books for Libraries Press.

Ledgin, N. (2001). *Asperger's Syndrome and self-esteem*. Arlington, Texas: Future Horizons.

Sacks, O. (1995). Prodigies. *The New Yorker*, Jan. 9, 44-65.

Chapter 1

Attwood, T. (1998). *Asperger's syndrome: A guide for parents and professionals*. London: Jessica Kingsley Publishers.

Autism Research Institute (www.autism.com).

Autism Society of America (www.autism-society.org).

Bauman, M. L., & Kemper, T. L. (1994). *The neurology of autism*. Baltimore: John Hopkins University Press.

Cesaroni, L., & Garber, M. (1991). Exploring the experience of autism through first-hand accounts. *Journal of Autism and Developmental Disorder, 16*, 169-187.

Center for the Study of Autism (www.autism.org).

Courchesne, E. et al. (2001). Unusual brain growth patterns in early life in patients with autistic disorder. *Neurology, 57*, 245-254.

National Institutes of Health (www.nih.gov).

Mayo Foundation for Medical Education and Research (www.mayoclinic.com).

Chapter 2

Alert Program (www.alertprogram.com).

Autism Research Institute (www.autism.com).

Banker, S. (2003). *Personal interview. Children's Therapy Group.* Overland Park, Kansas.

Baron-Cohen, S. (2000). Is Asperger Syndrome/high-functioning autism necessarily a disability? *Development and Psychopathology, 144,* 1288-1292.

Coleman, R. S., Frankel, F., Ritvo, E., & Freeman, B. J. (1976). The effects of fluorescent and incandescent illumination upon repetitive behaviors in autistic children. *Journal of Autism and Developmental Disorders, 6,* 157-162.

Covey, S. (1990). *The seven habits of highly effective people.* New York: Simon Schuster.

Grandin, T. (1995). *Thinking in pictures and other reports from my life with autism.* New York: Vintage Books

Hardy, P.M. (1989). National Conference of the Autism Society of America. Seattle, Washington, July 19-22 (personal communication).

Hartman, T. (1994). *Focus your energy: Hunting for success in business with Attention Deficit Disorder.* New York: Pocket Books.

Huggins, J. (1995). *Diagnostic and treatment model for managing SIB, rage and other hyperadrenergic behaviors in autistic/PDD and DD populations.* Aurora, Ontario, Canada: Kerry's Place.

Irlen, H. (1991). *Reading by the colors.* New York: Avery.

McKean, T.A. (1994). *Soon will come the light.* Arlington, Texas: Future Horizons.

Narayan, S., Moyes, B., & Wolff, S. (1990). Family characteristics of autistic children: A further report. *Journal of Autism and Developmental Disorders, 20,* 523-535.

Ratey, J. et al. (1987). Autism: The treatment of aggressive behaviors. *Journal of Clinical Psychopharmacology, 7,* 35-41.

Williams, D. (1992). *Nobody nowhere and somebody somewhere.* New York: Time Books.

Williams, M. S., & Shellenberger, S. (1996). *How does your engine run? A leader's guide to the alert program for self-regulation.* Albuquerque, New Mexico: Therapy Works.

Chapter 3

Autism Society of America (www.autism-society.org).

Bureau of Labor Statistics, U.S. Department of Labor. *Occupational Outlook Handbook, 2002-03 Edition,* www.bls.gov/oco/.

Chapter 4

Bolles, R. N. (2003). *What color is your parachute? A practical manual for job-hunters and career-changers.* Berkeley, California: Ten Speed Press.

Kanner, L. (1971). Follow-up study of eleven autistic children originally reported in 1943. *Journal of Autism and Childhood Schizophrenia, 1,* 112-145.

Sinetar, M. (1987). *Do what you love, the money will follow.* New York: Dell.

Chapter 5

Benjamin, J., Stanny, B., & Duffy, K. (1995). *How to be happily employed in Kansas City.* Kansas City, Missouri: Career Management Press.

Chapter 6

Bureau of Labor Statistics, U.S. Department of Labor. *Occupational Outlook Handbook, 2002-03 Edition,* www.bls.gov/oco/.

Grandin, T. (1999). *Choosing the right job for people with autism or Asperger's Syndrome.* Center for the Study of Autism. www.autism.org.

Chapter 7

Career information for the profiles came from the U.S. Department of Labor's *Occupational Outlook Handbook* web page (www.bls.gov/oco/). This information can also be found in the handbook's paper version in library reference areas.

When to Disclose Autism or Asperger Syndrome to an Employer

People who have mild Asperger Syndrome and no obvious speech delay should concentrate on selling their talents when they apply for jobs in technical fields such as engineering, computer programming, scientific research or electronics. Technical companies often employ people with undiagnosed Asperger Syndrome, and it is likely you will fit in. There is no black-and-white dividing line between "computer nerd" and Asperger's Syndrome. It is a continuum, a matter of degrees.

If you need to modify your cubicle to eliminate fluorescent lights, you can disclose that fluorescent lights give you a headache and you need a quiet spot because too much noise and commotion interfere with your concentration.

However, if you get a job in the special education field, it may be an advantage to disclose a diagnosis of autism or Asperger Syndrome. People in this field are likely to appreciate your insights.

Individuals with high-functioning autism with more severe symptoms may need to disclose their condition to their employers. They need to make it clear what their strengths are and where their weaknesses lie. A busy receptionist job would be difficult due to all the multitasking. When you discuss autism with your employer, emphasize your strengths and the positive contribution you can make with your talents.

When Do You Disclose Your Disability – If Ever?

When do you disclose, if ever, to an employer? There is no one correct answer to that important question. If you do self-disclose, this information must be kept confidential by law. If you have questions about when to disclose, the following website lists some good ideas:
www.unbc.ca/disabilities/dismod1.html

Getting into fights with employers about your rights under the Americans with Disabilities Act may cause more problems than it solves. The legal route is the last resort. Getting into a nasty lawsuit with an employer may get you branded as a troublemaker. There are some situations when a lawsuit is justified, such as being fired after the boss lied to her superiors and told them that you failed to do your job even though you had good performance reviews. Just remember, if you choose to fight, even if you win the battle with an employer, others may be reluctant to hire you. You will be forced to choose between the lawsuit or a career.

The U.S. Equal Employment Opportunity Commission
Facts About the Americans with Disabilities Act

Title I of the <u>Americans with Disabilities Act of 1990</u>, which took effect July 26, 1992, prohibits private employers, state and local governments, employment agencies and labor unions from discriminating against qualified individuals with disabilities in job application procedures, hiring, firing, advancement, compensation, job training, and other terms, conditions and privileges of employment. An individual with a disability is a person who:

- Has a physical or mental impairment that substantially limits one or more major life activities;

- Has a record of such an impairment; or

- Is regarded as having such an impairment.

A qualified employee or applicant with a disability is an individual who, with or without reasonable accommodation, can perform the essential functions of the job in question. Reasonable accommodation may include, but is not limited to:

- Making existing facilities used by employees readily accessible to and usable by persons with disabilities.

- Job restructuring, modifying work schedules, reassignment to a vacant position;

- Acquiring or modifying equipment or devices, adjusting modifying examinations, training materials, or policies, and providing qualified readers or interpreters.

An employer is required to make an accommodation to the known disability of a qualified applicant or employee if it would not impose an "undue hardship" on the operation of the employer's business. Undue hardship is defined as an action requiring significant difficulty or expense when considered in light of factors such as an employer's size, financial resources and the nature and structure of its operation.

An employer is not required to lower quality or production standards to make an accommodation, nor is an employer obligated to provide personal use items such as glasses or hearing aids.

MEDICAL EXAMINATIONS AND INQUIRIES
Employers may not ask job applicants about the existence, nature or severity of a disability. Applicants may be asked about their ability to perform specific job functions. A job offer may be conditioned on the results of a medical examination, but only if the examination is required for all entering employees in similar jobs. Medical examinations of employees must be job related and consistent with the employer's business needs.

DRUG AND ALCOHOL ABUSE
Employees and applicants currently engaging in the illegal use of drugs are not covered by the ADA, when an employer acts on the basis of such use. Tests for illegal drugs are not subject to the ADA's restrictions on medical examinations. Employers may hold illegal drug users and alcoholics to the same performance standards as other employees.

EEOC ENFORCEMENT OF THE ADA
The U.S. Equal Employment Opportunity Commission issued regulations to enforce the provisions of Title I of the ADA on July 26, 1991. The provisions originally took effect on July 26, 1992, and covered employers with 25 or more employees. On July 26, 1994, the threshold dropped to include employers with 15 or more employees.

Job Tips

Keep in mind these job tips when you are searching for a job:

▶ Try to make sure the projects you work on have a well-defined goal or endpoint. For example: *design a system to handle 100 cattle per hour with no electric prod, or program a computer to do accurate speech recognition when a person talks fast.* An example of a poor way to assign a person on the spectrum to a project would be to say: "Your job is to build a new cattle handling system" or "Your job is to develop new computer programs." These instructions are too vague. You will decide how to do the design work or write the program, but the boss needs to be specific about what the facility or program is supposed to do. The desired outcome of the project has to be specific.

▶ Sell your work, not your personality. Whenever possible, make a portfolio of your work to show what you can do. Develop skills in things that other people want.

▶ Try to make sure coworkers, and especially bosses and supervisors, know your social limitations so they don't suddenly throw you into a complex social situation such as seeing important clients. If you feel it would be inappropriate to disclose our autism diagnosis, tell the boss you are a pure "techie" and that you do your best work at your computer and that too much non-technical work makes you nervous and frustrated.

Knowledge is power in the job search process and in the job itself. Remember to share what you know with others and to always ask questions when you do not understand something.

Further Readings on Interventions to Reduce Sensory Problems

Coleman, R.S., Frankel, F., Ritvote E., & Freeman B. (1976). The effect of fluorescent and incandescent illumination on repetitive behavior in autistic children. *Journal of Autism and Developmental Disorder, 6,* 157-162.

Elliot, R.O., Dobbin, A.R., Rose, G.D., & Soper, H.V. (1994). Vigorous aerobic exercise versus general motor training effects on maladaptive and stereotypic behavior in adults with both autism and mental retardation. *Journal of Autism And Developmental Disorder, 24,* 565-576.

Irlen, H. (1991). *Reading by colors.* New York: Avery.

Knivsberg, A.M., Reichelt, K.L., Hoien, T., & Nodland, M. (2002). A randomized controlled study of dietary intervention in autistic syndrome. *Nutritional Neuroscience, 5,* 251-261.

Lightstone, A., Lightstone, T., & Wilkins, A. (1999). Both colored overlays and colored lenses can improve reading fluency, but their optimal chromaticities differ. *Optholmic Physiology Optometry, 4,* 279-285.

Rosenthal-Malke, A., & Mitchell, S. (1997). Brief report: The effects of exercise on self-stimulating behaviors and positive responding of adolescents with autism. *Journal of Autism and Developmental Disorder, 27,* 193-202.

Stehli, A. (1991). *Sound of a miracle.* New York: Doubleday.

Walters, R.G., & Walters, W.E. (1980). Decreasing self-stimulating behavior with physical exercise in a group of autistic boys. *Journal of Autism and Developmental Disorders, 10,* 379-387.

Wilkins, A. (2002). Colored overlays and their effects on reading speed (a review). *Optholmic Physiology Optometry, 5,* 448-454.

William D. (1996). *Autism: An inside out approach.* London: Jessica Kingsley Publishers.

Further Readings on the Link Between Creativity, Genius, and Abnormality

Andreason, N.C. (1987). Creativity and mental illness prevalence rates in writers and first-degree relatives. *American Journal of Psychiatry, 144,* 1288-1292.

Baren-Cohen, S. (2000). Is Asperger Syndrome/high functioning autism necessarily a disability? *Development and Psychopathology, 12,* 489-500.

Donnelly, J.A., & Altman, R. (1994, June). The autistic savant: Recognizing and serving the gifted student with autism. *Roeper Review.*

Grandin, T. (1996). *Thinking in pictures.* New York: Vintage Press (Random House).

Grant, V.W. (1968). *Great abnormals.* New York: Hawthorn.

Ledgin, N. (2001). *Asperger's Syndrome and self-esteem.* Arlington, TX: Future Horizons.

Further Readings on Creativity

Luria, A.R. (1987). *The mind of the mnemonist.* Cambridge, MA: Harvard University Press.

Morris, B. (2002). Overcoming dyslexia: *Fortune* examines business leaders and artists who have gone beyond the limitations of dyslexia. [Electronic version] May 13. www.fortune.com

Persson, C.B. (1987). Possible biological correlations of precocious mathematical reasoning ability. *Trends in Neuroscience, 10,* 17-20.

Silberman, S. (2001, December). *Geek Syndrome – autism and its milder cousin Asperger's Syndrome is surging among the children of Silicon Valley: Are math and tech Genes to blame? Wired,* 174.

Wheelwright, S., & Baron-Cohen, S. (2001). The link between autism and skills such as engineering, maths, physics and computing: A reply to Jarrold and Routh. *Autism, 2,* 223-227.

West, T.G. (1991). *In the mind's eye.* Buffalo, NY: Prometheus
	Books.

Career Resources

Americans with Disabilities Act information
U.S. Department of Justice
ADA Home Page
www.usdoj.gov./crt/ada/adahom1.htm

Autism Society of America – Offers a wealth of information
	on its web page, including information on each
	state's vocational rehabilitation offices, an excellent
	source of assistance for those who need job training
	and other vocational assistance.
	www.autism-society.org

Bolles, R.N. (2003). *What color is your parachute? A practical
	manual for job-hunters and career-changers.* Berkeley,
	CA: Ten Speed Press.

Bureau of Labor Statistics, U.S. Department of Labor.
	Occupational Outlook Handbook, 2002-03 Edition,
	www.bls.gov/oco/.

Center for the Study of Autism – Has information by a num-
	ber of authors on its web page covering a wide vari-
	ety of issues. Also offers a lot of information about
	autism itself. www.autism.org

Clausen, J. (2001). *Too lazy to work, too nervous to steal: How to
	have a great life as a freelance writer.* Cincinnati, OH:
	Writer's Digest Books.

Community Services for Autistic Children and Adults – Offers
	a wide range of social, educational and psychological
	services for those on the autism spectrum. Operates a
	supported employment program for its clients, prepar-
	ing them to enter the workforce. Located in Rockville,
	MD, the organization was started in 1979 by concerned
	parents of adults on the autism spectrum.
	www.csacc.org

Edwards, P., & Edwards, S. (1999) *The best home businesses for
	the 21st century* (3rd ed.). New York: Jeremy P.
	Tarcher/Putnam.

Farr, J.M. (1994). *America's top jobs for college graduates* (3rd ed.). Indianapolis, IN: JIST Works Inc.

Farr, J.M., & Ludden, L. (2003). *300 best jobs without a 4-year degree.* Indianapolis, IN: JIST Works Inc.

Hartman, T. (1994). *Focus your energy: Hunting for success in business with Attention Deficit Disorder.* New York: Pocket Books.

Hausman, C., & Cross, W. (1998). *The complete small business sourcebook.* New York: Times Books.

iCanONLINE – An online community for people with disabilities; this web page has information about employment, money and benefits, issues and rights and a whole host of other categories. www.icanonline.net

Kestler, D. (Ed.). (2002). *Career information center* (8th ed.). New York: MacMillan Library Reference USA Group.

Meyer, R. (1999). *Asperger Syndrome employment workbook.* London: Jessica Kingsley Publishers.

Morkes, A. (Ed.). (2003). *Encyclopedia of careers and vocational guidance* (12th ed.). Chicago: Ferguson Publishing.

Morkes, A. (Ed.). (2001). *The top 100 fastest growing careers for the 21st century* (3rd ed.). Chicago: Ferguson Publishing Co.

Schaffert, T. (Ed.). (2001). *Exploring tech careers: Real people tell you what you need to know.* Chicago: Ferguson Publishing.

Parker, L.V. (1997). *How to start a home-based writing business* (2nd ed.). Old Saybrook, CT: The Globe Pequot Press.

Shulen, J. (1998). *Home-based business mom: A basic guide to time management and organization for the working woman.* Santa Barbara, CA: Newhoff Publishing.

Sinetar, M. (1987). *Do what you love, the money will follow.* New York: Dell.

Smith, M.D. et al. (1997). *A guide to successful employment for individuals with autism.* Baltimore: Paul Brookes Publishing Co.

Wright, J. W. (20001). *The American almanac of jobs and salaries.* New York: Avon.

Entrepreneurship

For information on entrepreneurship, try these websites. They offer concrete information about starting small businesses:

The U.S. Small Business Development Centers (www.sba.gov/sbdc/)

Kauffman Center for Entrepreneurial Leadership (www.entreworld.org)

Association for Enterprise Opportunity (www.shoga.wwa.com/~aeo/)

National Association for Community College Entrepreneurship (www.nacce.com)